I'm Telling!

I'm Telling!

Kids Talk about Brothers and Sisters

Edited by Eric H. Arnold
and Jeffrey Loeb

Illustrations by G. Brian Karas

A *hole in the sock* Book

Little, Brown and Company
Boston   Toronto

Text Copyright © 1987 by Eric H. Arnold and Jeffrey Loeb
Illustrations Copyright © 1987 by G. Brian Karas

First Edition

Some of the children's names in this book have been changed.

Library of Congress Cataloging-in-Publication Data
I'm telling!

"A hole in the sock book."
1. Brothers and sisters — Juvenile literature.
I. Arnold, Eric H., 1951–   . II. Loeb, Jeffrey,
1946–   . III. Karas, G. Brian.
BF723.S43I48   1987   158'.24   86-21509
ISBN 0-316-05185-3
ISBN 0-316-05186-1 (pbk.)

Designed by Trisha Hanlon
RRD-VA
*Published simultaneously in Canada
by Little, Brown & Company (Canada) Limited*

Printed in the United States of America

For
Adam, Benjamin, Jeremy, and Zachary
and for
Carol Hantman
E. H. A.

In Memory of My Mother,
Dorothy Lob
J. L.

Contents

Acknowledgments

We would like to thank all the young people who shared their experiences with us about "how they survive their brothers and sisters."

Our deepest thanks also to the following:

— To the children's book folks at Little, Brown for their support of this book and of Hole in the Sock.

— To our editor, Stephanie Lurie, for her encouragement, patience, and humor.

— To publisher John Keller for his continual support.

— To copy editor Doris Heitmann Collins for understanding and appreciating what kids have to say.

— To Maryclare O'Donnell, Sarah Guille Kvilhaug, and Lisa Miller for their good cheer.

— To Becky Goodwin in the New York office for her positive spirit and great promotion of our books.

— To National Public Radio's nightly news and features program "All Things Considered" for continually providing a home for Hole in the Sock features about children and children's issues.

— To Ted Clark, executive producer; Art Silverman, producer; and Peter Breslow, associate producer.

— To all the members of our Advisory Board who have supported us from the very beginning. They have given us excellent feedback, suggestions, and ideas: Terry Payne Butler, Peggy Charren, Tom Cottle, Dick Harris, Carolyn Hansen Tracy, Valerie Henderson, Gerald Lesser, Brad Spear, Dominic Varisco, John Welch, and Beth Winship.

— To Andrea Truax for her excellent word processing skills and ability to meet never-ending deadlines (always with grace and good humor!).

— To photographer Stephan Miller for his skill and generosity.

— Thanks to all the people who helped promote *Lights Out!* and who support Hole in the Sock: Fred Lown, Pat Cerame, Abe Herrera, Kathy Tatum, The Stone Environmental School, Judy Flam, Keith Arian, Terry Phinney, Lynn Dowall, Barbara Levitov, Margie Singer, Duane Bond, William Jordan, Mary Hirschfeld, Violet Spevack, Mopsy Strange Kennedy, Jan Bailey, Monitoradio, Maria Harris, "Kids America," Tom Bergeron, Judy Walcott, Julie Winston, Joel Rizor, Betsy Haas, Jane Glickman, Terri Payne Butler, Parker Damon, Hedy Lopez, Sara Stashower, Velma Stone, Sharon Milinsky, Evelyn Moore, Michael Wager, Karen Blaker, Steve Siegel, Sylvia Avner, Lynn Sygiel, Terrell Lamb, Steve Reiner, Terri Schmitz, The Dearborn School, Chuck Berk, Debra Stavro, Dave Derosier, Leslye Discont-Arian, Grey Bassnight, Esta Snider, and Sharon Baker, Linda Abrams, Jonathan Rothbart, Michael Tichnor, Carol McLaughlin.

— *Eric Arnold and Jeff Loeb*

— Thanks to Rochelle Solomon (my sister), Elizabeth Warner, Fred Lown, Jack Flynn, Tom Jefferson, Barbara Black, Angela Johnson, Irving Arnold, Bernice Lockhart, Kathy Wilson, Michael Romanos, Vickie Romanos, David Fuller, Sandy Siegel, Barry Shlachter, Amrita Shlachter, and Martha Vaughan for their encouragement and humor.

— *Eric Arnold*

Introduction

Does your brother or sister —

- Always tag along when you go places?
- Share special secrets with you?
- Constantly start fights with you? (Or do you start some of them?)
- Tell you funny (or almost funny) jokes?
- Use your stuff without permission (and break it)?
- Tattle on you about everything?
- Treat you fairly?

Do you ever wonder how you can survive your brother or sister?

We at Hole in the Sock interviewed kids on tape so we could learn more about how brothers and sisters get along (or don't get along).

We discovered that many brothers and sisters really *do* get along with one another. We also learned that in some families, they fight all the time and aren't very happy about it. And in other families, they seem to like each other one minute and not like each other the next.

This book was written for you by kids your own age. In their own words they share with you what it's like in their families and how they try to get along with their brothers and sisters. They talk about things such as how fights are started and how to avoid future fights, what it's like to share a room with a slob, and how it feels if a brother or sister tattles on you. Some kids even talk about the good qualities of their siblings!

So if you're curious about how *other* kids get along with their siblings, this book is for you. If you want to try to figure out how to better get along with your *own* brother and/or sister, this book can help. And even if you think your brother or sister is the greatest (most of the time), this book might remind you of the fun and special times you have together. We hope you enjoy what other kids say about their brothers and sisters in *I'm Telling!*

I'm Telling!

Sharing Stuff

"It takes a fight to share."

My little sister and I cannot share *anything*. Whenever we share something I think it's unfair, and she thinks it's unfair, until eventually our mother just comes in and splits it for us. We can't compromise, either. In fact, once, when we were having ice cream, my mom had to take the ice cream and put it on a measuring scale, each of the two bowls, to show we had the same amount.

— Todd, 12

Sharing's a big problem. Whenever I start playing with something, my little brother always has to play with the same thing. If I sit down and start watching TV, my brother will come and sit down. We have this kind of rule, our made-up rule; whoever turns on the TV gets to pick the channel. But the minute I leave the TV to get something out of the refrigerator, he gains control and he goes, "Okay, we're going to watch this." He usually really bugs me when he picks a channel, and he *knows* I don't like it, like basketball or something. I don't really like basketball. And he doesn't really like basketball. He just watches it to annoy me.

It's the same thing with toys. I mean, if I start playing with Legos and I build this really neat thing, and then I put it in the box because it's time for dinner or something, right after dinner he'll rush into the room and he'll go, "Oh, this is mine, this is mine, and I'm playing with this."

— Jason, 11

Whenever I ask my younger brother to use something, he always goes, "Well, I'm going to use it. I was just about to use it." And he never was, he was doing his homework or something. He shares most of the time, but not always.

— Lenny, 11

My brother and I usually fight over the bathroom in the morning and so we get punished by not getting to watch TV at night. Sometimes it's his fault. He always splashes me with his wet brush and his toothbrush and everything. And even if *he* does it, *I* get in trouble.

— Lisa, 12

My sister and I fight over the living room because there's a desk that I work at to do my homework. My father built her her own desk in the other corner, but she always takes the big one anyways and says she was

there first. So I end up sitting at this tiny desk that she has over in the corner, and it's not fair because the desk is hers anyways.

— Sophie, 13

We don't really get along with sharing. I wear her clothes and she wears mine, but it takes a fight to share. And when she has friends over, I'll go sleep on the couch so her friend can have my bed.

— Tobé, 13

We usually don't share things. I mean we *take* things, but not with nice words. The only thing that we sometimes share is friends. I work with my brother's friend at the store on Saturdays instead of my brother working with him, so they won't talk. But you know, I'm getting to be friends with him and stuff like that. And my brother's friends with my friends.

— Cindy, 13

Sometimes, if my little brother wants to play with an action figure I have, he'll ask if he can play with it, and then if I say no he sits there and waits. He finds the right moment. When I put it down to pick up another guy, he grabs it, and he runs away up into his room so he can play with it. Then I end up chasing him. And then eventually he starts crying because I either took it away, or I got so frustrated with him I hit him so he'd let go of it.

I have to read to him every night. So he shares his books with me and I share my books with him.

— Jonathan, 11

My older sister, if we buy something that we have to share, a week later she'll say it's hers. This is just an example: Say we got, I don't know, just a toy or something, a week later she'd say it's hers and not ours. It really gets me mad because she says, "No, I'm in charge of it. It's mine. You can't use it right now." And I get mad because I helped pay for it or something, and she just takes it over.

— Rebecca, 10

My older brother and me always have a problem with the TV changer all the time, especially when my parents leave. It'll be lying around or something and all of a sudden I'll move really quickly to grab it, and he'll grab it right before me, and I get all mad. We always get in fights about what channel we should watch. We always get in *big* fights about that.

— Nadine, 10

My younger brother is eight, and his name is Ben. I don't want him to share my things because sometimes he wants to wreck them, and sometimes he just loses them. He's a very good person that loses stuff. One time he lost a dollar for his hot lunch. He lost it on the road. And there was a lot of wind so it blew away. He came home and started crying at my mother. My mother got real mad.

— Cassandra, 13

I have a younger brother and he doesn't share at all. If he gets something out for himself, like milk and cookies or something, he doesn't ask me if I want any. He just puts it back away and says, "Go get it yourself." He's just a pest.

— Emily, 12

If I get something, like, say I go to a birthday party, and you know how you get little bags with the stuff in them and everything, well, one of my sisters is really greedy, and whenever she comes back with a bag, and she's got stuff in it, she never shares with me. And then when I get something she just says, "Courtney, well, you never share with me, and I *always* share with you."

— *Courtney, 10*

When my mother buys new clothes she says that me and my sister have to share it. Then my sister goes and wears it all the time. She doesn't even let me wear it. The other day my mother bought a belt, and my sister takes it right up to her room, and she puts it in her drawer.

— *Shari, 12*

If there's something like food or something like that, I always end up with the biggest piece because my brother thinks that — my little brother — he thinks if you're six you should get six cookies. So I'm twelve, he thinks I should get twelve cookies. So I like it that way.

— *Heather, 12*

Annoying Habits

"My sister chews everything she sees."

I kiss and hug my little sister too much and she says, "Yuk! I hate your kisses!"

— *Karen, 10*

I bother my younger brother sometimes. Well, sometimes I annoy him in different ways. It depends. Like, I have level 1 annoyance, level 2 annoyance, level 3 annoyance. Level 1 annoyance isn't quite that bad. It's just, you know, poking around, giving soft pinches. Level 2 annoyance is tripping him when he runs down the hall or something, and level 3 annoyance is jumping all over him or doing something really drastic.

— *Carol, 11*

My sister's annoying habit is that she chews everything she sees. She's almost eight, and she still does it. She used to take Barbie dolls and chew their fingers off, stuff like that. And she used to eat the Legos. And she used to take my action figures, and she'd chew on their hands, maybe rip off their heads. And just the other day we were watching TV, and I saw her chewing on a piece of plastic or something that she found somewhere. She just chews on everything. So my mom has to go on a gum-buying binge. And she buys every single type of sugarless gum. And we always have gum in the house. Stacks and stacks of gum.

At night I come in late into my room to get ready for bed, and I turn on my light, and my sister always yells at me. She says, "Turn off the light! Turn off the light!" Like last night I went in and turned on the light and she goes, "Jason, turn off the light!" And I didn't really want to because I couldn't find my dresser. And it kind of gets annoying because I *want* to have the light on. And she never sleeps anyways. I think she tries to stay awake. And I think that's kind of unfair.

— *Jason, 11*

I have this younger brother who sleeps in the same room with me. We sleep in bunk beds — he sleeps in the lower bunk, and I sleep in the top bunk. And we switch around once in a while. Anyway, he has this real funny habit of stuffing all his stuffed animals at the end of his bed so there's a big space. And then he rocks. He goes, "nih-nih-nih-nih." He makes so much noise because our bunk beds creak all over the place; they were banging all against the wall. One time, when he was a little kid, he started rocking, and his carriage went halfway across the room. That's one of his bad habits.

— *Matt, 12*

Sometimes my sister, she runs around the hall singing, "Strawberry Shortcake" and stuff, and I'm trying to do my homework, and I yell at her and then she goes, "Mom, Kenan yelled at me." And it really annoys me when she does that because, I mean, I can't do my homework when she's singing "Strawberry Shortcake." Or sometimes I go in her room and she says, like, "Don't laugh," or something. And I laugh just to annoy her. Because I'm mad at her.

— *Kenan, 10*

I do annoy my three sisters, and if all of them are talking I come in the room and start listening, and they go, "Get out! Get out of here right now!" They push me out of the way and go, "No!" and slam the door in my face. They always do that.

— *Kenya, 11*

My sister is very annoying. We have problems with the phone. Like, the phone will ring and I'll pick up the phone. I'll say, "Hello," and they'll say, "Is Rachel there?" and I'll say, "Yes." Then a second later my sister'll pick up the phone and say: "Rachel, I have to use the phone." When I'm off the phone, she never needs the phone. *Ever.* But it's just when I'm on the phone, *she* always needs the phone. I tell her, "Why don't you use the phone now because I don't have to?" She only has to when I'm on it. It drives me crazy.

— *Rachel, 12*

My sister always uses crying to get me in trouble. She is *so* emotional. Any little thing will set her off. Then my mother will start feeling sorry for her, and then I'll get in trouble. She does that all the time. It drives me crazy.

— *Sophie, 13*

At dinner my brother always chews with his mouth open on purpose, and it always bugs me. I always yell at him, and then my mother says, "You're not his mother." And that really bugs me.

— *Lisa, 12*

My little sister has a very annoying habit of when she finds something lying around she always either rips it up or scribbles all over it. And so I come home, find my homework with her name written backwards on it, and I feel like I could just kill her.

— *Karen, 10*

My brother snores *so loudly.* Even though our rooms are across the hall from each other, I can hear him. And he breathes *so loudly.* And it keeps me up all night. It's even worse when we have to go to hotels together because he's only eight and we sometimes share a double bed in the hotel, and when he turns over I wake up in the morning with his arm in my face.

— *Jill, 12*

My younger sister has a habit of barging in at times when I would like to be by myself, and I find that is very annoying because I have very little time to myself. She demands a lot of attention, and she expects a lot out of me because I'm older. She looks up to me. Oftentimes, when we get into arguments, I pull rank on her. I usually take advantage of the fact that I'm older, and I use what I know against her — such as, I would know vocabulary she doesn't know and could insult her or use a different language to insult her because I take Spanish. So it's an appropriate way to get back at her.

— *Kate, 12*

My older sister, she used to always suck her thumb even though she's a lot older than me. She stopped sucking her thumb when she was twelve years old. It used to always annoy me because everybody used to always complain to her about sucking her thumb. And she never stopped. She'd always go into a corner or something and do it in private.

— *Mark, 12*

Okay. I have an older brother who's eighteen, and he's going to college next year, and he's very bossy. If I'm in the shower, he wants me to get out for him. Or get off the phone for him. He can be nice, but he likes people to revolve around him. He wants people to buy things for him, like food. And if he puts it on the shopping list, then that's his. He locks his room because he thinks people go in there all the time and get into his stuff. He's annoying.

— Erica, 13

My older brother turns on his stereo at night, and he's right across the hall from me. And he turns it up wicked loud, and I can't get to sleep until about eleven thirty because the thing's so loud. And I'm, like, "Uuuuuuhhh! I can't get to sleep! Shut that thing off!" I'm screaming at him. He just keeps it on. He can't hear me.

— Matthew, 12

Sometimes my brother, he figures he can get attention by whining or crying. So if I have something he wants, then he cries for it, and then my mom turns around. But it backfires on him because my mom gets really annoyed at him, and he gets in trouble instead of me. Actually we *both* get in trouble because she usually screams at the two of us.

— Jonathan, 11

I have an older sister, and she always asks me to, like, help her with her homework, to dictate stuff she has to write out or type. I sometimes stutter or something, and she gets really mad at me. And it just aggravates me because *she's* the one that asked for help. And she just gets all upset.

I just stop helping her and just leave.

— Laura, 12

My parents always have the radio on, and so my brother, he mouths the words. My brother, when he's in his bedroom, plays a rock station. And he stands in front of the mirror while he's brushing his hair, and he sings and mouths the words, and he really, really annoys me. He does it just because he knows I don't like it. Sometimes he has food in his mouth, too. That's annoying.

— *Randy, 12*

I have an older brother, and he watches pro wrestling. And he always tries out the wrestling moves on me. He says it won't hurt, but it always does, and so it's really annoying.

— *Erin, 11*

Whenever I'm sleeping in my bed and I have to wake up, my younger brother brings in the dog, and it jumps on my bed and wakes me up and licks my face.

— *Tony, 11*

See, I usually have to do my hair first in the morning because it's very hard to brush out. And my younger brother, who has short hair, he hogs my brush. He takes my brush, he goes in the bathroom, and he locks the door. And he just goes over the same spot a million times. A million times. I'm like, "Derek, hurry up because I have to use the bathroom, and I have to do my hair, and it's time to go to school," and he never lets me use it because he's always doing his hair in one spot. And he just does that by purpose because he doesn't want to let me use the brush. He does it by purpose.

— *Deidra, 11*

Sometimes my sister, when she eats, she takes about a half an hour, and the food gets cold, and I have to look at her eating. That's an annoying habit.

My little brother has an annoying habit of leaving his bed undone when he's going to school and I have to do it before I get home because I don't want to get whacked. I *do not* want to get whacked. I don't like him getting hit either because it kind of makes me cry.

— *Teodolinda, 13*

One annoying habit that my brother has is he doesn't listen to me. Like, if I tell him something that I know is right, he won't listen to me because he says boys don't have to listen to their sisters. And that gets me mad because I feel that he doesn't ever want to listen to me.

— *Tanya, 12*

My brother Troy, he's my older brother, every time somebody calls, he has two girls on a line, and he always wants me to make the decision who he wants to talk to.

We have a two-way line. And one girl's on one line, and the other girl's on the other line. And he always is wanting me to make the decision, and I don't like that.

— *Dora, 12*

One of my sister's annoying habits is when my mother goes out she thinks it's party time, so she brings in all the friends that she isn't even supposed to play with because of the habits they have. And then, like, they'll say, "Oh, what's this?" and it's something of mine, so she'll just give it to them, and then they'll go home with it.

— *Colleen, 12*

My brother goes out and every single day he comes back rotten dirty. How does that happen? He's a pig. He goes out and he rolls in the dirt! And he comes back and flicks it all over me. And then he takes a temper.

— *Melody, 12*

My younger brother picks his nose. That's annoying.

— *Danielle, 12*

My stepsister cracks her knuckles a lot, and it's very annoying. I block my ears sometimes. I tell her to stop. It doesn't work.

— *Peter, 12*

My sister always talks on the phone, and when I want to get on it, she always says, "One more minute. One more minute." Then, "Two more minutes." And it goes on and on. And then finally I get the phone, and sometimes it's too late.

— *Paul, 12*

My brother has the bad habit of throwing all his smelly socks around the house. And my sister has the habit of messing the house. Me, I have the habit of cleaning. But that's the end of my habit. That's it.

— *Anne, 12*

Good Points

"She tells me all the gossip of the seventh grade."

Usually my brother's a pest, but sometimes there're days that we have together when we're just the best friends in the world. On those days he always sticks up for me. Always. Whenever I do something wrong, it's, "She didn't do it. No." He does have some good qualities.

— *Jill, 12*

The best quality my little sister has is that she's really little so she can't bother me. She's two. And she's funny. She just says funny things. But my younger brother, I don't know. He really doesn't have very many good qualities. Except he's not around very much.

— *Molita, 12*

The only good quality about my younger brother is that he's a good basketball player. He likes sports and all that. So I don't have to be alone when I play basketball.

I could play against him. That's nearly the only thing that he's got going for him.

My older sister, she's seventeen. She has some good qualities, not too many, but the majority. She comes home on her curfew. She's very polite. And if she doesn't like something she doesn't say, "Oh, that's awful," or, like, "I don't like it," or something. She respects how people . . . what they feel and stuff. She doesn't — if there is something wrong with someone, she doesn't stare at them. She's just very nice.

— *Eli, 13*

My younger sister's good to talk to. When I have a problem that I don't want to tell anyone, like my mom, especially (because she's slightly overprotective, and I sometimes don't want to talk to her), I'd rather talk to my sister instead, and I say, "If you tell, I'll kill you." And then she says, "I'll kill you back." So I say, "Fine. But don't tell anyway."

I'm doing a Japan map now, and she's always wanting to help, like, "Oh, can I find a city for you? Oh, please, please, please." It's helpful. She's very artistic, too, so sometimes when I have trouble drawing things she helps me a little bit.

— *Janine, 13*

My older brother does things for me sometimes. He tapes things for me. Sometimes he lets me borrow money, but he usually makes me pay it back with interest. He gives me a certain amount of time, and if I don't pay it back, it's, like, a quarter every day or something.

— *Andrea, 12*

I guess the best quality of having an older sister is that she can drive you places. My sister works at a restaurant, so every now and then I get free food, but not often.

Every now and then she's okay. She understands my problems when I have them.

— *Bob, 13*

My brother is seven, and I'm thirteen, which is six years difference. (I can do math.) We get along real well usually. He tries to find out what other people are feeling, and he notices — like, his friends will be talking about this school thing, and he'll say how his friends are picking on his other friend, and he'll stand up for his friend because he feels bad for him. He really tries to look into the other person's side of the story, and tries to make people feel better. He doesn't always do it, but he tries.

— *Julie, 13*

My younger brother is eleven, and he's probably, like, my best friend because we do everything together. We collect coins, comic books, and baseball cards, and we go fishing and on trips.

— *Matt, 13*

Both of my sisters watch wrestling, and they know who everybody is, so I can talk to them about it and stuff. They also tape all the wrestling so, if we get into an argument of who won this match or who got it or something, you can always watch the tape.

— *Michael, 11*

The thing I like best about my older sister is — well, maybe not best, but I like a lot of things about her — but one thing is she can tell me all the gossip of the seventh grade. Then the thing I like about my younger sister is that it's fun to help her do her homework since she's in third grade. I mean, it's fun to help younger kids do things. It makes you feel good.

— *Liz, 11*

In the car, when we usually go on trips to the grocery store or something, I get car sick a lot. I like my nose "done." In the car I'll lay down in my sister's lap, and she'll massage my nose.

— *Shayne, 11*

My older sister is very pretty, and every time she goes to the bathroom to get dressed I look at myself, and I'm all dirty and everything, and I say, "How come you're pretty and I'm ugly?" And she says, "You're not ugly, you're pretty too."

— *Laura, 10*

The best thing I like about my brother and sister is they're smaller than me and I get to mind their business and all that. I get to hit them sometimes, and sometimes I like them because they're nice and sweet, but some-

times they don't listen. Sometimes they listen. That's the best part, they listen a little bit. And my little brother, he's five, I like him because he's so cute and cuddly. Sometimes he beats up little kids that I'm not supposed to beat up because they're smaller than me.

— *Teodolinda, 13*

If I have a problem with something, my little brother will listen to me, or if I need a shoulder to cry on, he'll let me cry on his shoulder or something. He's real nice. And when he's sleeping I like when he's wiggling his ear, or he covers his face with the covers, and I like to go in there and give him a hug and a kiss and tuck him in for bed.

— *Tanya, 12*

The best thing about my brother is, sometimes if I'm in a hurry or something and my room's all messed up, and my mom wants me to clean it up, he cleans my room for me.

— *Geoffrey, 12*

I like my brother around because, like, when my parents go away or something, and if either one of us gets scared, the other one is always there. We kind of help each other with little things.

Once we were in the middle of a big thunderstorm, and my parents weren't home. They came home a couple of hours late, and we got really scared. We thought something was going to happen — the power was out and we didn't know *what* was going to happen.

We help each other through things like that.

— Heather, 11

My brother, he's younger, and he always has a lot of money, and he buys me stuff sometimes. It's weird. He'll be fighting with me and then he'll go out and buy me something, like, if I'm in a store and I want it, he might get it for me.

— Jennifer, 11

The thing I like about my little sister is that she's so small and sweet, and every time I come home she always runs to me and gives me a kiss.

My brother sticks up for me and stuff. That's the thing I like about him. Like, if anybody ever starts bothering me, he goes up to them and says, "Stop bothering my big sister."

— Anne, 12

My older sister has a lot of good qualities. She's very caring and she's really nice. When she has a friend over, and I don't have a friend over, she always lets me talk with them and play games with them and stuff like that. She's nice. She's mean once in a while because that's typical, but most of the time she's really nice.

— Melissa, 12

I have a younger brother. And the thing that I like about him is that he's pretty strong for his age, and we can wrestle, and he won't get hurt too badly.

— Joel, 11

I guess some of the good qualities of my older siblings are that they know right now what I'm going through or I have gone through in my past years. There's also an older sister — I guess when she was my age she was a lot like me. There's comparing, but we also tend to see the good sides. I guess they say, "I went through that, too." So they understand.

— *Jennifer, 13*

Oldest, Middle, Youngest

"Being the oldest sort of stinks."

I'm the oldest in my family. It's good and it's bad. I get a lot more responsibilities. Well, my mom won't say that, but I think I have more responsibilities than my brother, but he gets off the hook a lot. Whenever I do something bad, it's still, "Go to your room." Whenever *he* does something bad it's, "Jeff, it's okay. But don't do that next time."

— *Jill, 12*

I don't like being the middle because my little sister, she's only two, and she gets all this stuff and everything, and I don't get nothing. My big sister gets everything just because she's in high school. So I don't get nothing. Well, I get stuff, but they get more, and they get treated better.

— *Stan, 12*

Being the youngest means I get everything I want, because when I go to the store I pick something and hide it behind my back, and my father says, "What've you got there?" And I say, "Nothing, nothing!" And he says, "Just put it in the cart." So I do, so I get it. But my brother likes the game Monopoly and he wanted to get it. But because my father had bought me and my brother desks, he didn't have enough money to buy him the Monopoly game. So my brother got real mad and said, "Why do you always buy her something and not me?" My father had already bought the desk and some clothes for him, but my brother still said that he didn't get nothing and I did, so I got mad. But he still didn't get the Monopoly game, so I got happy and mad at the same time.

— *Felicia, 11*

I'm the youngest one in our family. There is just my older sister and myself. She's fifteen. I like being the youngest. It's fun. I mean, you don't get as much atten-

tion as people always say you do and everything, but I like having an older sister, because when I'm having problems in school, or I need help with my homework, she's always there, and she always knows what to do. It's easier to have an older sister. Sometimes I wish I was the oldest so I could have power over everything, but my sister doesn't take advantage of being the oldest.

— *Rachel, 12*

Being the oldest is hard. You've always got to do everything, like, when your sisters are young, and your mother's, like, "You've got to show them how to read and how to do their homework." You've always got to do everything around the house. When they're young they don't do anything because they don't know how to. That's why I would like being the youngest, because you get everything.

— *Nina, 11*

I'm the oldest. I always get blamed for everything because I should know better. My brother, he's ten, and I'm twelve. Two years from now I'll still be getting blamed for knowing better, and my brother, when he's the age I am now, he won't get blamed for things. It's not fair to say that Ben, my littlest brother, is not old enough to know better because he *is.* That's what my parents were telling me when *I* was six, I should know.

— *Heather, 12*

I think that being the oldest sort of stinks.

— *Julie, 12*

I don't like being the youngest because they can boss you around, and plus I get blamed on everything, and they do it all. And because they're bigger, they think that they can push me around.

— *Kiernan, 11*

I like being the oldest because I get to boss my sisters around all the time. But there's one thing I don't like. All the time my little sister — she's four — she always falls on purpose or trips or something when she's near me and starts crying, and I just get blamed for it.

— *Jason, 14*

I like having an older sister because she does most of the work in the house, and I hate having a younger brother because he does none of the work in our house. I like having a younger brother because I can pick on him, and I hate having an older sister because she gets to go more places, and then I get jealous of her because she gets to go to so many places.

— *Jennifer, 12*

I'm the oldest in my family and sometimes I feel sort of mad at my brother because he gets away with some of the things I think I could never get away with when I was his age. He gets to do everything earlier than I used to. That gets me so mad, but my mother doesn't listen.

Sometimes it's better being the oldest because you get more responsibility — well, not more responsibility, but just, like, more privileges.

— *Danielle, 12*

I'm the second to youngest. I have two older brothers and one older sister and one younger sister. I like the position that I have because, even though I'm second youngest, I have a lot of power over my sisters since I'm a boy in the family, and our family doesn't have too many boys. So when we go to, say, away on trips, I have more power than them, and I get to do better things because I'm a boy, so I think that I'm pretty lucky. And because I'm the youngest boy, people treat me a lot better. Like, when we go away they say, "Oh, you look so cute," or whatever. They always notice me first.

— Craig, 14

I like being the bigger brother because I get to slave my younger brother around — tell him to do all this stuff, and I have some control over him. It's just nice to have that responsibility, I think.

— Wei, 11

I am in the middle. I have one older brother and two younger brothers. And one of the pluses is that I get my own room because I'm an only girl. Some of the minuses are that my three brothers — they're kind of wild sometimes — they're always fighting, and sometimes they go into my room and take things.

— Allison, 12

I have an older brother. I get to have anything I want.
I get to get him in all this trouble, blame stuff on him.
We get in fights, and he gets in trouble for punching me,
but I don't get in trouble for punching him.

— *Claudia, 13*

Fighting

"Between me and my brother, we can fight about anything."

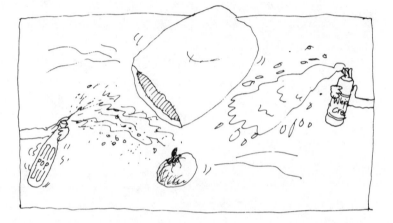

Between me and my brother, we can fight about anything. Whether it's food fights, pillow fights, anything. Just anything.

— *Brad, 12*

My younger sister, whenever we're, like, sitting down, we have a Coke machine up in our loft, and we take Cokes out of it. We're only allowed one Coke per day. Anyway, we'll be sitting in the beanbags playing video games or something, and she always has the habit of either going in front of me or in back of me . . . and the Coke always falls out and lands on my lap, okay? And so then she refuses to clean it up, and all the ants come rushing across my lap, okay? And then she just sits there like she didn't do anything.

Then Mom comes up, and Mom starts cleaning it up, and I say, "Well, Margo did it." (And she always does it.)

And she goes, "Oh yeah, blame it on the younger one all the time." And so I walk off in a storm, march off to the bathroom, get a towel, and I don't even wet it or anything, and just slap it on, and Mom yells at me again. So I march off towards the bathroom, and I get it wet. And I clean up the whole mess. And I sit there, and I think about how mean my sister is and how I always get all the blame.

And then I wonder about other kids and what they think about their sisters and brothers.

— Nicole, 11

A couple of weeks ago I was sleeping and my brother said, "Theo, you gotta go to school." I said, "I'm sleeping still. I want to sleep for a while. Ten more minutes." And he goes, "Get up." And so he went in his room. And I'm wondering, "What's he gonna do?" So I went back

to sleep. About thirty minutes later he came in with something like a bugle. You know, those things they have in the parades? He had that, blew that thing in my ear. I got up, went "Whoa!" Then I ran after my brother, and he went in my father's room, and he goes, "Dad, Dad, Dad, get up!" And my father woke up like that! Then my father said, "What are you's doing?" I was out of the room, I was waiting for him, I was behind, like, a wall. And when he came back out I grabbed him, and I took the thing and threw it out the window. And my little sister went downstairs and grabbed it. He got it back, brang it back in. So I took it again without him knowing, and I put it in the trash, and then I took it downstairs and threw it in the dumpster. Didn't get it back again.

— *Theo, 12*

My older sister tells me her secrets and stuff like that. And it's good because, you know, you hear a lot of brothers and sisters who get in fights a lot. Like, around New Year's we were going, "Well, we've got to keep it below four fights for the year." Last year we got four. And all those four were around that time because that's when we got out the Scrabble game.

— *Annie, 11*

My younger sister, whenever we get in wicked — well, strong — fights, she starts punching, and I strike back, and she misses. So I start laughing at her. And she gets so hysterically mad that she starts cracking up. I don't know why. She cracks up and rolls around the floor, and she comes over and gives me a big, wet kiss. And so then we're friends again.

— *Nicole, 11*

If I'm trying to do my homework, my little brother will come in, and he'll take his sock off, and he'll try and smother it in my face. So I pick up a glove, and I shove the sock in, and I hit him over the head. And then it always ends up he runs and tells after a little bit.

— Jonathan, 11

My biggest problem about fighting is that my brother David likes to fight me a lot and doesn't listen when I tell him to stop. And because he's a bit bigger and much better wrestler, he usually winds up on top, so that's a pretty big problem. And eventually I wind up usually a little bit hurt, physically. So I'm not really enthusiastic about wrestling with my brother or even fighting.

— Daniel, 11

I remember one fight when I didn't like my mother's supper, so I said I was sick. My oldest sister was going to play tennis with her boyfriend, and I love tennis. And she kept on saying, "Well, you're sick. You cannot come." And I was really, really mad because of that. And I was starting to say, "Well, I hate you," and all these terrible things. Finally, we both got over it. But she ended up going to play tennis without me.

— Layne, 11

My father's dog was in heat. She's a Doberman and by accident I let her out, and so she mated with not a Doberman dog. (Because we know this dog, he's a Doberman, and these other people own it, and so we usually breed her to him so she'll have nice, good puppies and everything.) So I let her out, and she got really bad puppies, I guess. My brother, he kept annoying me about it, like, saying that it was all my fault, and it was really stupid and everything. And he made me feel real bad. Worse than just my father, because that's his dog, you know. Sometimes he'll rub it in.

— Randy, 12

I get in a lot of fights with my older brother because he tells me what to do, and I say, "No, I don't think I

want to do that," and he says, "You *gotta* do it." One
time he almost threw me across the room because he
was so mad at me. He said, "Hey Matt, why don't you
go clean up the room?" And I said, "No, I don't want to.
It's fine." He said, "Clean up your room!" I said, "No."
So he threw me across the room a few times. Then after
a while I learned, "Hey Matt, you gotta *do* something
about this." So I finally stuck up for myself and I got
beat to a pulp.

— *Matthew, 12*

My brother beats me up sometimes. He's younger
than me — he's eight. And sometimes I can hurt him,
but it's sort of in the verbal range of fighting. I'm much
more advanced than he is. Except in physical I can get
badly wounded because he's very strong. And the TV
gets him hyperactive. He'll go around, and he'll, like,
jump on top of my head if I'm watching TV because he's

hyped up from the TV or sugar or something. So we get into fights about that.

— *Emily, 12*

My younger sister likes to boss me around. And one time I was really sick of it. So I said, "Robin, will you please be quiet?" And she said, "No!" So I just kept asking her, and she said, "No! No!" So she came over because my parents weren't home, and she said, "I'm the boss of this house!" and shoved me against the wall. And so we just had this big fight. Glasses were breaking, the lamp fell over, the bulb broke. We just waited until my mother got home.

— *Ben, 11*

A long time ago my brother insisted that I come with him. It was snowing out that day. He's three years bigger and older than me. His friend just gave him his idea. I saw him go over to my brother, and he goes, "Hey Mike, why don't you jump on your brother or something? Maybe you can beat him up or something." I know, his friend wasn't very nice. And my brother lifted me up with almost one hand (but he had to use the other) and threw me right over a fence. And I hated it. He was *so mean* to me! So I punched him in the nose, and his glasses broke. And I almost had to pay for the glasses until my mom heard the whole story.

— *Tim, 10*

My brother, he had broken his toe once, and so, even with a broken toe, he was playing on the bed with my cousin. And my cousin stepped on his toe, and I was standing near my cousin, so he blamed it on me. He got up, and he slapped me. I just got back, and I punched him in his face. So we started fighting, and I hit him hard, and then I really did step on his toe, and I said, "That's good for you because at first you shouldn't have blamed me, you should have looked at your cousin because your cousin was playing. I told him to stop because he was going to step on your toe. At least I *cared* about your toe, and you just got up and slapped me, so I had to punch you." He didn't want to listen to me, so he was mad at me for a couple of days. And then, at last, he said, "Yeah, you were right. I was wrong to blame you and slap you."

— Rudi, 12

My brother is nine. And he has this wicked bad temper. He starts a fight over everything. I'll say the sky is blue, and he'll say it's green. So then he'll scream, "It's green!!!" And then he'll start throwing things and trying to beat you up. He picks up a ball and throws it at you. He picks up everything and throws it at you. How does it end? My mother comes in, "What's going on?!" And I get in trouble. Every time! Every single time *I* get in trouble.

— Melody, 12

When me and my older brother get in fights, I usually just start yelling and screaming because I just can't stand it, and then I tickle him to death. He tries to tickle me, and it doesn't work, so I always win, and he gets mad at me and backs off and runs outside. I'm not ticklish. Only my father can tickle me and make me laugh.

— Leslie, 11

Sometimes my sister's bothering me, and I yell at her, and she says, "Well, you should just ask me nicely." And I go, "How can I ask you nicely if I'm already angry at you?" And then we just start yelling at each other. My mom sends us both to our rooms, and we have to stay there. But I don't mind because I just do my homework, and she has to stay in her room so she can't bother me.

— Kenan, 10

I fight with my sister because sometimes she wants me to deliver messages to her boyfriend, and I always say no, so she gets mad and we start fighting.

— *Brad, 12*

We fight about things like, who has the bathroom first in the morning, or who gets the shower first, or who's to practice first or feed the dog or walk the dog. We've never really fought over major things. Sometimes we have sort of little ongoing warfares. One time she put some pump hand soap on my toothbrush, and I proceeded to brush my teeth, and I had very clean teeth for the rest of the week, but I was not amused. But we always make up. Usually one of us will go into the other person's room. We usually flee to our rooms afterwards. And one person sort of comes on a peace walk. They come down the hallway to the other room, and we stand, we talk, and we apologize.

— *Kate, 12*

I have two little sisters, Martha and Adalina. They're always fighting over little things, like, if one sister has something in her hands, the other one says, "It's mine!" Then my other sister, "No, it's mine!" So they fight. Then they become friends again. Then they start fighting again. And they come running to me, they say: "Deanna, she did this." I say, "Get out of here. Don't come near me because I don't want to be in the middle." Anyway, they never pick a fight with me because they know what's best for them.

— *Deanna, 14*

Sometimes my sister, well, she wants me to deal with her problems. Like, one time her friend was over, but she didn't want to do anything with her, so I had to tell her friend that she wasn't home, and the friend saw her up in her bedroom. And I had to deal with getting rid of her friend. And after that I got mad at my sister for putting all the pressure on me. And that caused a fight.

— *Seth, 12*

My brother doesn't really care too much about me. He just fights with me for no reason sometimes. He uses me as a punching bag. I don't know why. Sometimes I don't want to make up. My brother just comes over to me and asks me if I want to play basketball or something.

— *John, 12*

My brother and I always fight about what we want to watch on TV. Like, if my brother wants me to turn off the VCR, and I want to go to sleep early, he makes me stay up and go downstairs and get things for him so he doesn't have to get out of bed.

— *Andrea, 12*

What usually starts a fight for us is if we're cooped up in the house on a rainy day, and we start to notice something that we know the other person is really embarrassed about, like thumb sucking or something. We'll tease the person about it because there's nothing else to do and start getting into fights. My mother usually splits us up because she doesn't want us to make noise in the house because she's in the house, too.

— Sophie, 13

My brother and I usually get in fights because he is so annoying. Every day: "Robin, come on, let's play ball." "Jimmy, go play with your sister, go play with Rebecca." And he's always, like, "No, come on. Let me play with you." And so whenever I do he usually cheats because he's five, and so he doesn't really know about cheating. Whenever we tell him that he's wrong, he's always, like, "Well, I'm right." So that really gets on my nerves. And we usually don't make up like, "Oh, I'm sorry." But he usually rushes into his room, I go into mine. And then we just all of a sudden start talking to each other like nothing ever happened.

— Robin, 12

Me and my sister always fight because she goes into my room, she throws garbage all over the place, she takes my lipstick, my perfume, and everything. She rips something from my wall, she tears out my wallpaper, she writes on the wall. I smack her a couple of times, tell her to get out of my room, and she doesn't listen, so we get into a big argument or fistfight. Oh, sometimes she asks me for a favor, and I say, "Okay. This is the only favor I'm going to do for you. Next time you do it yourself." So then we start talking. We start playing games.

— Marisol, 13

Once my brother really got mad at me and I said, "Let's calm down and talk this over a little." He didn't really want to do that, but I said I'd give him half my chocolate bunny rabbit from Easter. I gave it to him, and then he asked me if I had any more, and we were real friends for about five hours. And then, the next morning, he comes into my room. I hate to say this, but he put my hand into a bucket of warm water. Do you know what that does?

— *Tim, 10*

Once I told my brother to let me use his Walkman and he said no. And I begged and begged him. I said, "I'm going on a trip so I need a radio." Then he said, "Would you buy me twenty-five pieces of candy?" I said, "No!" Then he said, "All right, then you're not going to get it." I said, "All right, all right." Then, that day, I brang him only ten. And he said, "Where's my other fifteen?" I told him that I didn't have enough money because I wasted it on the trip. Then he started screaming at me. He said, "I'm never going to let you use that radio again!" Then I said, "I don't care. I'll get my own." So I did.

— *Felicia, 11*

One day we were in the room playing this game, Monopoly. I was winning. I had more money than my brother, and I was the banker. So he got mad, and he said I always steal the money out of the bank. And I said, "I didn't steal any money." But I had taken one hundred dollars because I needed one hundred dollars, right? And I said, "This says you could borrow money from the bank." He said, "No it doesn't. Where?" He couldn't read that good, so I showed him this word, and he couldn't read it, so he said, "All right, all right." So then I said, "That's right. I *always* win." So he said, "All right, cool."

So at the end of the game I was counting my money. He just picked up my money and threw it in the box so I couldn't count it anymore, because he knew I had more money than him. And I had stolen all his land, bought all this and that. He didn't have anything.

— *Tanya, 12*

Me and my sister have a good relationship. Sometimes we fight but most of the time we just, like, sit down and talk. We have a real good time. We don't usually play tag. But it's more of a nice conversation-type relationship. We really love each other. So it's pretty nice having my younger sister.

— *Amy, 11*

I don't have brothers and sisters, but most of my friends do, and it seems that it's okay to fight sometimes. Most of my friends who have brothers and sisters, even though they fight, deep down they still love each other. And so I think you just have to try to respect each other's property and stuff, and that kind of thing. But you *have* to fight sometimes. It will always happen.

— *Ivy, 12*

Babysitting

"I hold the fort down 'til my mom comes back."

Whenever any of my older sisters babysit, it's usually really, really fun. We pop, like, one hundred . . . well, that's a little exaggerating, but we pop a lot of popcorn and put on tons of butter and everything and get a whole can of soda, and we're having a real fun time, and we watch all our shows, and we play some games. It's really fun, though, because none of them yell at me or anything, and I don't have to go to bed really early!

— *Layne, 11*

We have three different TV's in our house, and since there's only two kids, me and my big brother, we have cable, and we go into a different room and use the TV's. So we don't really talk to each other much, and we each take care of ourselves. Sometimes I get a snack or something, and he wouldn't know about it, and sometimes he gets a snack, and I don't know about it.

— Jason, 11

When I babysit my little sister, we usually stay downstairs and watch TV. If I go upstairs to get changed into my pajamas or something, she practically waits outside my door while I'm getting changed. She must think that, like, someone's going to come up and murder her or something. When she's upstairs, and I want to go downstairs, she wants me to wait upstairs so that she can come down when I come down.

— Todd, 12

Sometimes when I'm babysitting my little brother, we'll usually watch TV. Sometimes we'll play a game or something, but if I'm really hooked up in a TV show, and it's time for him to go to bed, I'll just say, "Oh, forget it," and I let him stay up a little bit later. Right when the TV show ends, I rush him upstairs so my parents don't get home and find him awake.

If my parents are going to be out for just an hour or two they'll let me babysit, but if it's going to be longer than three hours, they'll usually get a babysitter. When the babysitter comes, it's, like, they really don't do anything. They just sit and talk on the phone, and I end up watching my brother. So my mom's paying the babysitter for wasting our money on our telephone. *I* should be the one that gets paid!

My little brother got his foot caught in the door one time, so I tried to get him out. We couldn't get it unstuck. It was like his pant leg was caught in it. He was stuck in the bathroom, and I was stuck outside. I forced the door open, and he sprawled backwards, and he almost fell into the toilet. It was open, too. He *almost* fell in, but he didn't. Too bad.

— Jonathan, 11

Whenever I babysit my younger brothers and stuff they always fool around and do all these bad things just because my parents aren't there. And when I tell my mom about it, they say, "No, no. He's lying." They start going crazy. They start beating up each other. They make huge messes, and then I have to pick them up. I asked them to make popcorn, and then they started throwing it all over the place. They get all crazy and everything. And then, when my parents get home, they get mad at me for not taking good care of them when it really wasn't my fault because they were going crazy, and I couldn't stop them.

— Adam, 11

Sometimes my oldest brother babysits me, and he's a real pain because he doesn't let me do anything. He says, "I'll make you go to bed early" if I do something that he doesn't like. And he always makes me pick up after myself because he goes, "I'll get in trouble if you don't." I just don't really like it when he does that. I try to cooperate with him, but sometimes it's very hard because he's my older brother. I mean, they're kind of a pain sometimes. And he's at that age (fifteen years old) where he always yells names at me and calls me "Bubba," and he calls me fat and stuff.

— Greg, 11

I get babysat by my older brother, and he gets paid by my parents, but I don't think it's fair because he goes into his room and listens to music and talks on the phone, and I watch TV. So it's just like he's not even there and I'm not there. So I don't see why he gets paid for it.

My parents are trying to work out something so when he's not there, to let me stay at home alone more because I'm getting older, and also when he is there to have him try to know what's going on more.

— Sarah, 11

Usually, all the time when my sister babysits me, we have a really fun time. We go up there in my mother's bed, and we watch TV, like, four shows in a row or something. Once, when my mother and father went out to dinner, we put Hawaiian Punch in a big bowl and served it with ladles and put on the radio full blast and had a real fun time.

— *Vanessa, 10*

I babysit my sister sometimes. She's nine years old, but she acts like a baby. Believe me, she does. So when I babysit her, she takes all her toys, and she throws them all over. I tell her to pick it up, and she gets an attitude, and so I gotta hit her. Then I hit her, and my mother gets home, and she tells her that I hit her for no reason. But first she picks up the toys, though, before my mother gets home. Then she tells my mother that she didn't do anything, while I knew that all the toys were all over the floor, and so I get in trouble. My mother yells at me, I yell back at my mother, my mother yells at my sister, and then she finds out the truth.

What I *like* about babysitting my sister is that she's company. She keeps you company. If you feel like playing a game, she plays a game, but she's a sore loser.

That's what I like and hate about babysitting my sister.

— *Rudi, 12*

I babysit my little brother, Kevin. I like babysitting kids, but I like babysitting my baby brother most because he's fun. But, he gets bad, and he'll start calling you all these swears. Like, if you're watching TV, and you're not paying more attention to him than you're paying to TV, he gets mad and tries to poke you in your eye so you pay attention to him. One day I was watching TV, and he started throwing things at me. I was looking around, but I couldn't see him. I said, "I must have imagined something." So then he threw this thing at me that hit me in my head. I was looking for him, but I couldn't find him.

— *Tanya, 12*

I don't mind babysitting my brother, but he likes to pretend that he doesn't need a babysitter and he acts up. He just goes off and leaves and doesn't tell me. Then I get in trouble because I didn't find out where he was going or anything. He just leaves the house and goes to his friend's house. Then I end up going outside and looking for him. Sometimes I get him home before my parents come home. Other times my mother doesn't really get mad at me, but she gets mad at my brother really bad. She gets really mad at him. Then he sneaks extra time. He's supposed to be in the house by 8:00, but he comes in later because he thinks, "Oh, my sister's babysitting me so I can come home any time I want."

— *Jennifer, 12*

I like babysitting, but sometimes my brother and sister, they take advantage of it. I only babysit at night, usually. They always jump on the furniture and everything. I tell them not to, but they keep on doing it, and sometimes, like, I get really mad with them, and I just put them to bed because I'm so mad. Then they'll go downstairs because my grandmother lives downstairs, and they'll tell her, and she'll come up and say, "Well, stop doing this, and stop doing that." I get really mad because she's really not the babysitter, because *I* am.

— Jodi, 12

Sometimes I have to babysit my younger brother for about two hours or so. After my mother leaves he's okay for about an hour, and then he starts getting all mean and stuff. He starts hitting, and then finally I ask a friend over. We send him up to his room, and then he takes a tantrum. First he won't go up the stairs. Then we try to carry him up the stairs, but then he starts kicking. When we get him up there, he tries to open the door, but we hold it shut. Then he just sits there screaming. Then we leave. Then he gets tired and goes to sleep in his room.

— Stephanie, 11

Whenever we have a babysitter, my little sister always says things that either aren't true or are exaggerated like anything. First she asks the babysitter what she had for lunch and all this stuff. And then she says, like, maybe we had soup that day, "Oh, I ate a gallon of soup. I was so hungry, and now I'm full, but I can still eat." It's weird. She exaggerates. The babysitter knows it.

— Alyssa, 10

Sometimes I babysit my younger brother, who is five — he just recently had a birthday — and my other brother, who is nine. But every time my mother leaves me in charge, my brother who is nine always gets mad and says, "No, I'm in charge, not you! And if you're in charge, we're both in charge!" So we really get into a fight. So when my mother gets home she pays me and sends my brother to his room.

— *Michael, 12*

I babysit my sister when my parents go out. It's on weekends because, like, Monday or Tuesday or on the weekdays I go to bed at nine o'clock. On Friday or Saturday night my parents will go out, and it depends, like, if they're out until three o'clock I won't babysit, but if they're out just, like, 'til ten or eleven I'll babysit her, and we don't get in fights. We always stay upstairs and are sort of scared of the dark to go downstairs. We don't get in fights. We just eat and watch TV.

— *Leah, 11*

I hate to babysit, especially when I have to change my brother's diapers because it's disgusting and I don't like to do it. When he was younger I didn't like to feed him either because he threw it all back out. Now I don't have to really do that because my grandmother's at home.

— *Susan, 10*

Sometimes my mother goes out somewhere, and I hardly ever go with her because I have to babysit. Sometimes I want to make a cake, and they pretend they're sleeping. So I go make a chocolate cake, just for me. A big one. And, then, as soon as it's all done, I take it out. They wake up and start eating it, and I get all mad and stuff because they keep doing it.

— *Miguel, 11*

It's easy to babysit my brother and sister because I already know how they are. I like babysitting, especially at night. When they bug me I turn off all the lights, and I turn off the TV, the radio, and everything. I make sure there's no light in the house, I close the curtains, and I put them all in one room, and then we start sitting down in the corner, and I try to get my sister scared. We go up to my room, and I try to get her scared, and then she doesn't want to go out into the hallway, or she doesn't want to pass the line in my room. She doesn't want to leave or anything. I have to pick her up and take her downstairs. I never get paid, but my parents, they take me out to the amusement park or to the movies or for Chinese food or something like that. That's the way they repay me, but it's fun.

— *Marisol, 13*

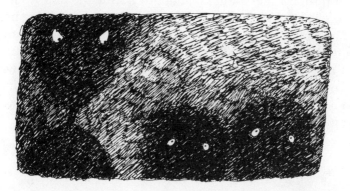

I never babysit my brother because he's too old, and he babysits with me. Sometimes when he babysits with me we babysit my little sister. Sometimes we'd get in fights, and he'd be too loud so I tell him to shut up. Then he starts telling me to shut up. Then Lauren will wake up, and we don't know what to do, so we both go upstairs, and we try to put her back to bed again. Then we start talking to each other again. So, whenever she wakes up we kind of come together because we have to help, we have to cooperate.

— *Rebecca, 13*

I always get stuck with babysitting my sister. Even if I want to do something that night, like go out to the movies with my friends, I still have to stay home and babysit my sister. Whenever I babysit she tries to aggravate me, to make me feel bad, like, she says, "Ha, ha, Terry, you didn't get to go to the movies."

— Terry, 12

My fifteen-year-old brother usually babysits me, and he usually stays downstairs, and I usually stay upstairs, and we avoid each other. He doesn't hit me or anything.

—Andrea, 12

I make fun of my little sister, and she starts crying, and then I feel a little bad about it, but she annoys me. She'll do something awful, like when I'm babysitting her, she's on the couch, and she falls over and puts her hands on the floor, and she says, "Help me, Nina, I'm falling!" I go, "No way! You're not falling! If you can get down, you can get up!" Then she starts crying, and I go, "Fine, I'll help you." And she keeps on doing that over and over again.

— Nina, 11

Sometimes it's hard when I have something else planned, and then I have to cancel it because my mother says family comes first, and I have two younger siblings. That means I get stuck with babysitting when sometimes I want to go out. But sometimes it can be fun, because, like, when she pays me, that's extra pocket money and stuff like that.

— Jennifer, 12

I know some of my friends, if it's inconvenient for them to babysit for their younger brothers, then they get paid for doing it — except when I babysit, my mother says that it's a responsibility, and I'm his older sister, and I should do that, and she tries to work around my schedule if it's something that is inconvenient for me. My brother's actually in a stage right now, where he's very afraid to be alone, and he always follows me around wherever I go. It's very annoying, and I had screaming fights with my mother about it. She just says that he's getting better, and I don't think he is.

— *Emily, 12*

I hate babysitting because my brothers and sister don't listen to me. They play around, throwing bottles inside the house, playing. They mess up the counter, *everything* in the house. When my mother comes she finds her house a mess. She gets mad at me, because I'm the oldest, I'm supposed to take good care of them. They just don't listen. They go tell my mother, and I get mad.

— *Noel, 13*

Sometimes when I babysit for my mother, she tells me to hold the fort down 'til she comes back.

— *Brad, 12*

I usually don't have to babysit my brother because I think he's kind of old enough to take care of himself. But when he needs babysitting I babysit him — but it's not official babysitting. He usually watches TV. See, my mom doesn't tell me to babysit. I just hang around him so he doesn't get in trouble.

— *Ali, 12*

It used to be that last year when my mom needed a babysitter, she'd say, "Jill, you're babysitting." But this year, since a lot of people ask me to babysit, we have a little arrangement. If someone calls me first to babysit, but my mom needs me, I still have to babysit for my younger brother, but then I get paid a regular amount. But if no one calls me, and she needs me to babysit, then tough luck.

— *Jill, 12*

When I babysit my six-year-old brother, at the start
he'll be real good, and within five minutes he looks out
the window to make sure everyone's gone except for
me, and he'll start saying things like "doggy, doggy," and
he'll try riding our kitten. I have to try to stop him because he's almost killed the cat. He's had the cat eating
string, which really, you know, will rip them up.

I give babysitting reports. I've only had one good time
babysitting my brother. That's when my sister was here
helping me, too. Every five minutes I'd have a report,
and I'd write it down in a little notebook — I'd give him,
like, A's, B's, C's, D's, and I skipped all the others, except
for Z. I went down to Z –. He's only had one C once, and
he's never gotten any better than that.

When my brother's riding our poor little Siamese kitten, the kitten will look up to see if he stopped, and
within two minutes, if he hasn't stopped, the kitten will
roll over on his back, open his mouth, put all his claws
out, and stick his arms up in the air and try climbing
my brother's back or something. And he has plenty of
holes in his back. Then I come up. And usually I just
say, "Julien, I'll give you another thirty seconds to be
good." And he comes back at me and says, "You bungy,

you." So I sit him down in the chair, and I say, "Julien, you be good or I'm never babysitting you or giving you another birthday present or Christmas present in your life." He then is good.

— *David, 11*

Tagging Along

"...I always wanted to be with the big kids."

I always used to tag along with my brother because I was little, and I didn't like to go to school, and I always wanted to be with the big kids. And so I just used to tag along with him and his friends and annoy him by doing that. But now I don't anymore because I really don't care what he's doing.

— Kim, 12

Sometimes if my brother has maybe baseball practice, or if he's going to a friend's house that I know, I'll go along. He doesn't really like it, even if I don't go in or anything. Even if I just go and walk with him. He doesn't want to be seen with me because he's in tenth grade.

— Robert, 12

My brother's younger than me, and when I go to parties he always wants to come along. Like, one time I was going to go to a birthday party, and we were going roller-skating, and my brother wanted to go really, really a lot. And he was really a baby at the time — now he's seven — so my mom said, "All right, we'll take him, and we'll go rollerskating with him, okay? We'll take him, and you have a good time at the birthday party."

Well, what I think is when baby brothers or sisters come along, it's not as fun because you're always looking after them as if it's your job, but you don't really like to. It's just something that you do instinctively. And that birthday party was kind of embarrassing for me because my brother was there at the rollerskating place, and my brother was kind of, you know, embarrassing me a little bit.

— *Wei, 11*

When I was younger, everybody in my class used to like my older brother. I don't know why, but they used to like him, and they used to think he was so great. So I would try to tag along after him so that I was so great, too, so I'd be popular also.

— *Leslie, 11*

Sometimes when I can't find anything to do, and my older brother runs off with his friends and stuff, I like to follow him, just 'til I find something to do. He usually has fun things to do. And there's a farm down the road, and I go down there by myself, and he goes down there by himself. And you know, sometimes he goes down there, and I happen to be going down at the same time, and he thinks I'm following him. Well, sometimes I am. And he gets mad at me and calls me a bunch of things. So my father said, "Well, if he calls you anything just tell me, and I'll take care of it." I don't follow him anymore. I find my own things to do.

— *BJ, 13*

When somebody comes knocking on the door for me,
like Bayleen or Dottie or Lordez, you know, my friends,
or a boy, we'll go to a store somewhere, and my sister
always likes to tag along: "Oh, take me to the store with
you, do this and do that." And I'm always saying, "Ma,
can't I do anything in peace?" And she goes, "Well, take
her along, she's the littlest." I always take her. I always
tell her, "Don't ask for anything 'cause I ain't got no
money." And she goes taking cake, ice cream, anything
she wants. And the guy gives it to her, free. That's embarrassing, tagging along with a little pest.

— *Marisol, 13*

Whenever I go to a party, my mom makes me take
my younger sister with me, and when I'm talking to my
friends she comes over, and she starts taking my friends
away from me, so it ends up that I'm here alone, and

my sister is talking with *my friends.* It's sometimes very embarrassing.

— *Stephanie, 12*

I stay close behind my older sister so I don't get lost. But I think she gets mad because she doesn't like to talk around her friends with me there. She doesn't know if I'm going to say something to my mom that I'm not supposed to know around school. Like, one time she got chained to her locker. I don't know if I was supposed to tell or not.

— *Nancy, 12*

Whenever her friends aren't around or something, my older sister will invite me to go for a walk down the street, or to see where they're building the houses, or to play basketball or something. And when her friends are around she'll just say, "Go away."

— *Laura, 12*

When I have a friend over, my youngest sister, Sabrina, tries to follow us everywhere we go. And it's very awful because she giggles and hits us and kicks us and throws rocks and stuff like that. It's okay because my friends like her a lot. But it's awful for a big sister to have a little sister following us guys around. I just tell her, "Well, Mumma wants you." Or a joke or maybe, "There's cookies in the house . . . Mom's baking some." And that gets her back in the house.

— *Cassandra, 13*

My little brother is always tagging along with me and my friends because we like doing a lot of stuff. And we say, "No, no, it's not something you'd be interested in." And he says, "Yeah, yeah, I want to come with you." And I say, "Nah." He never likes the stuff. And he finally realizes after hanging around with us for a while, "I do not like this." But I *never* hang around with my older brother. I have nothing in common with him other than being a relation. I do not like *anything* he likes other than his drawings.

— *Matthew, 12*

Whenever my older brother goes someplace with his friends, sometimes I have to go along. And they're always telling me to leave them alone and stop doing stuff with them. And one time we were visiting in Florida, and my cousin came, and he and my brother are really good friends. They were swimming and wouldn't let me within two feet of them. It was really bad. Well, I stayed away because they were calling me names, and they wouldn't let me in two feet, or else they would splash me or dunk me under.

— *Erin, 11*

My youngest brother, when I have a friend over, follows us into the room. And he brags about his age. And then he starts, like, doing some dance steps. And then he starts annoying us, and he won't leave. No matter what we do. Even if we bribe him. Oh, I give him a pack of gum. He just says, "No, I want to play with you."

— *Shelly, 10*

Whenever I have a friend over to sleep over, my sister always comes in and says, "Well, if I say one little word you can make me leave." Well, she always talks and stuff. And when we want to go outside or something, she always comes, and I can't get rid of her. She just follows me. She pretends like she's just playing by herself and says, "I would have came out here anyway."

— *Alyssa, 10*

Tagging with my sister is hard because she doesn't even like me walking to the store with her. Even when I walk behind her in the house she gets mad. She tells my mother that I'm too little for her. My mother says I'm not. So my mother has to pay her to take me out.

— *Andrea, 12*

Say I have to go to the store, and I want to get back fast because I want to go somewhere or something, my little sister will go, "I want to come to the store," and my mother will say, "Take your little sister. You never take her." So I have to take her. It takes a half an hour to go down the street.

— *Stan, 12*

Tagging along goes both ways. I don't know why, but I go with my brother, even just in his room with his friends and stuff, or to the movies or bowling or something. He doesn't like to be seen with me because now he's a teenager, and he's in junior high, and now it's more of a thing not to have your little sister around. But when I have somebody over and he doesn't, he can't find anything to do, so he just always comes in my room and bothers us, and you can't really ask him to leave because he won't, and so it works both ways.

— Sarah, 11

Being Compared

"... My sister's a big princess and I'm a little demon."

Sometimes I get compared to my older brother. Like, everyone always thinks he's really the nicest boy in the world or something when he's at school. I'm probably the only one that knows what he's really like underneath all that. He's really a monster, and he yells all these names at me. I mean, he screams. I yell back at him because I *gotta* yell sometimes. He never listens otherwise.

— *Greg, 11*

I have a problem because whenever I do something little or big wrong, and someone tattletales or something, my parents will go and give me the long, boring speech. And they'll say things like, "Look, Julien wouldn't do that." Or, you know, "Your sister wouldn't do that. She's only nine." They compare me a lot to my little brother and sister. And sometimes they'll compare my brother to our cats. We have two cats. And, you know, sometimes he can be so bad they'll say, "Look, those two cats — our cats wouldn't do that, even."

— *David, 11*

I get embarrassed because when I'm on the phone and somebody's calling for my sister, they go, "Is this Shelly?" That's *her* name. And I get all mad because I don't like to be called Shelly.

— *Tyler, 11*

Once at church my sister was going to be in the church choir (I was with my dad) and somebody from the choir was asking, "Are you the one that can sing so well?" And my dad said, "No, no. She's not the one. It's her older sister." And I felt so bad! I go, "Dad! Wait a minute! I can sing pretty well too." I got really upset at my dad, too.

— *Aileen, 12*

Sometimes I feel like my parents compare me with my sister, because you get that kind of feeling when they look at her, and they give her all the smiles and everything. And then they look at me and they — I don't know — they give me the cold shoulder sometimes. Then other times I think my sister feels that way.

— *Shayne, 11*

My brother always eats his vegetables. And I *never* eat my vegetables. And my mom *really* compares me with my brother. She goes, "Look at Mike over there. See him? He's eating his vegetables perfectly fine. Now why can't you do that?" And I'm here, "Uuuuh, well, uuuh . . ."

— *Tim, 10*

In second grade, my sister was the teacher's pet. And that was really hard because it was like, "Laura did this. Laura did that." And, "Oh, I remember the time when Laura did something like this." And so I think that was the year when I tried really hard to get better than her so the teachers wouldn't be saying that. They'd be saying it to *her.* They'd be saying, "Oh, your younger sister's really smart," instead of saying, "Your older sister's smarter."

— *Claire, 12*

My older sister is really small, and when we were little we looked so much alike, everybody thought we were twins. We both *hated* it because she was so much older, and she liked to be older than me, and I liked to be younger than her. And so we would always get mad and go, "No, we're not twins!"

— *Stephanie, 10*

My mother compares me to my cousins and my step-sister. Like, if my room's dirty, my mother will say, "I bet your sister's room ain't dirty." And I'd be like, "Ma, you always compare me with somebody!" And she says, "I'm not comparing you, I'm just pointing out a point to you." I say, "No, you're not pointing out no point to me. You're just comparing me to my sister. But who's the one that makes better grades, me or her?" And she says, "The grades don't matter." I say, "It matters to me because who's going to get a college degree? Me, right?" Then she'll shut up. And I say, "I clean up my room when I want to clean up my room." Then she don't say nothing else.

— *Tanya, 12*

I get compared a lot to my little sister because we wear braids and stuff and she's got little cheeks. They're always saying that I look like my sister, that I act like my sister. I don't act like my sister. And they're always saying that me and my sister keep dirty rooms, which is not true. Every time my sister does something wrong I get blamed for it because they say that we look alike.

— *Rudi, 12*

My mother likes comparing me to my big sister and says that my sister's a big princess and I'm a little demon. She says, "Your sister's prettier than you. Why you always got to run outside and be a little tomboy and run and get yourself hurt all the time? Your sister's always the big pretty one and she always takes care of herself. Why you always got to be the one who messes up yourself?"

— *Dora, 12*

Last month my mother said, "If you can save money like your brother, you can have one hundred dollars in your bank to buy a bike." Then a month later, my brother spent all the money that he had on games and eating, right? Then *I* was saving money. Then she said to my brother, "You should save money like your younger brother." See? That same thing.

— *Tommy, 11*

Well, my parents are always, like, "You're both good in sports, you're both good in school, you both look alike." And I don't like it because they're always comparing me the *same* as my brother, and it's not fair.

I wish I were different. I don't want to be the same. But they don't make me feel like I'm different. They make me feel like I'm the same.

— *Lenny, 11*

Once, when I was in a shop with my father and my brother, this lady that knows my father said like this, "That's your daughter? She looks so pretty. But look, that's your son. You can't compare them two." Then I told my brother, I said, "See? You're uglier than ever!" Then he started saying, "That lady only said it to make you feel better." I said, "No she didn't." Because everybody nowadays is saying I'm pretty. He gets jealous.

— *Felicia, 11*

All my older sisters are either in college or out of college, and mostly they'll always think of me as their younger sister and not, like, really who I am. So I get kind of aggravated when everybody says, oh, how great my older sisters were. They only think of me as their younger sister and not really me.

— *Layne, 11*

My mother always starts to compare me to my younger brother. When I come from school I take my clothes off, and I throw them around, and she comes and says, "I wish you were like your younger brother Chris because he never throws his things around." I say to her, "Well, Mom, he's the smallest one. He doesn't go to school and stuff." And then she says, "Well, still, you should be like him." And I say, "Well, Mom, how could I be like a little kid? What do you want me to act like? You want me to act like a little baby so you can give me the bottle?" So she starts getting mad. And I say, "Okay, Mom. I'm sorry." And when I go to bed I say, "Mom, I want my bottle!" Then she starts cracking up.

— *Bernard, 13*

Chores

"My brother gets all the easy work and I get all the hard."

Usually my younger brother helps me bring in the wood and my sister does other chores. And we don't really fight that much doing chores. We sort of work together, get it over quicker.

— *Tyler, 11*

The chores I have in my house are: one week I have the dishes, the table, and the oven to clean. My sister has the floor, the refrigerator, and the bedroom. Sometimes I do all three of my chores, and she does all three of hers. And sometimes she doesn't do any, so I have to do it for her. Last week I finished all my chores, and she didn't finish hers, and my father made *me* do her chores because she was doing her homework. And Monday I made her do mine instead of me doing hers.

— *Teodolinda, 13*

With chores I have a problem because my brother has a thing he likes doing. He likes my room. (I don't know why, because my room is just the same as his.) So he takes all his things into my room; he'll play with them, throw them around before he leaves, and walk out. And he always has to make sure he has somewhere to go. He'll go outside, maybe he'll be invited to a friend's house or something, so that he won't be here by the time I find out about this. So I'll come home and I'll look at my floor and I'll see a couple little baby books or things like that. So I go downstairs and tell my mom, "Julien messed up my room." And she'll say, "Oh, well it doesn't really matter." And she'll say, "Why don't you just clean it up, okay? It won't be that bad." She hasn't seen any of the messes.

— *David, 11*

Every time we have to clean up our room, which is about once a week, my mom tells us to go up, and we do it. Then — my brothers are sitting on the bed playing around with each other, just throwing everything all over the place — and I'm sitting there cleaning it up, and then I find another big mess. They go over somewhere else, make another mess. So it takes me, like, two hours to clean up.

—Adam, 11

I have two older sisters that are living at home, and we have to do chores, like, we have to feed our dog. Usually my older sister says, "Well, I have a whole lot of homework. You two do it." And that really gets aggravating because she usually never does. And we have to stack wood, too. And during the winter I usually bring it in. One sister helps, and the other one always says that she has homework. And she does, but she can take a little time off, I think, to help.

— Laura, 12

This is one of the most unfairest things, I think, about having a younger brother: He makes a big fuss, and sometimes our mom lets him off. I sometimes wash the dishes, I say, "Well, how come Jonathan doesn't have to do it?" "Well, because he doesn't know *how* to wash dishes." I think that doesn't make sense at all because what skill does it take to wash dishes? And she says, "Well, maybe he'll make a mess." I said, "Why doesn't he try it?" And so he had to be taught how to wash dishes, and now he still gets away with not doing it because he has homework to do. He saves homework for the time after dinner so he gets away with more stuff.

— Emily, 12

I have a younger brother. And sometimes I have to go get the laundry from the basement. My brother, he never does it because he says he's not strong enough to carry it up. My father says, "Oh, Joel, you do it." So then one time I made my brother do it; I said I would beat him up otherwise, and so he went. But he argued and argued. And my father said, "Yeah, Joel, he's too young." And then *I* had to go.

— Joel, 11

I have two older brothers, and my mother pays them twenty-five dollars to clean the stairway and make it all clean and everything. They do it, like, once a month. But when I do it I only get five dollars, and I do the same thing. I get mad at them but I don't say it.

— Leslie, 11

I have divorced parents. My father and mother are very different. When we go to my father's house, my brother gets the advantage even more than when we're at my mother's house. My father has his own company, and we were doing this stuff for him to put papers in numerical order. Jonathan was doing the same thing we were. And he kept going upstairs and getting food and everything. And I said, "I don't think you should pay him as much as you paid me because he did not do straight work. He was fooling around all the time." My dad said, "Well, he's younger. He should get a privilege to do that." He shouldn't have paid him at all. He was going up, he was wrecking things more than he was helping. I think that's truly unfair. Sometimes I wish that I could tape record what happened so I can prove it.

— *Emily, 12*

The thing I hate about chores is that since you're the oldest in the house, you have to do harder things. My brother gets all the easy work and I get all the hard. Like, I do the dishes and he'll put them away. And, like, I'll sweep, and he only has to take out the garbage. He gets just as much as I do, and I think that's unfair. And my sister even gets a dollar for messing the house. My mother just gives her money for nothing. Because sometimes she feels left out when we get money. She's a little brat. She's only four.

— *Anne, 12*

Every time when I come home from school, like, if I want to meet with this boy after school, my mother will be always finding something for me to do. And I'll be saying, "Why don't you let Elliot do it?" She says, "No, no, no. Elliot got a broken arm." I say, "Well, both arms ain't broken on Elliot. Just one arm's broke." She says, "So what? He can't do certain things." I say, "But it's not my fault he broke his arm. He should be able to do something." So then she says, "Go do the dishes." So I do the dishes. Then she says, "Take something out for dinner." And I take something out for dinner. So now she got a new job. I have to do *everything* now. I have to cook and clean and all this stuff.

— *Tanya, 12*

I have problems with my chores at home because, since I'm the oldest, my mother always makes me wash the dishes when she's doing something else. And when I go to wash the dishes, and I see my brother and my younger sister sitting watching TV, I get mad because I think they have to do something, too. When I finish washing the dishes, I go over, turn the TV on where they're watching, and I change the channel. Then my mother comes and calls me to do something else. And I say, "Mom, why don't you pick Chris or Shawn?" And then my mother says, "Well, they're younger." And I go over to them and say, "Why do you always have to be younger, why couldn't I be the youngest one," and slap them over the head.

So my mother calls me and she says, "Now you gotta go to the store." And I say, "Mom, can I take Chris with me so he can help me carry the groceries home?" She says, "No, he's too little to go with you." I say, "Can't I just rush him so he can get older?" And then my mother says, "No, just go." And I always get mad.

— *Bernard, 13*

My older sister and I, we either have to set the table and take out the garbage, or feed the dog and clear the table. And we always fight over when we're going to switch because neither of us want to do either job. So we're always fighting over that. I always have to clean my room and she never wants to clean her room. Her room is really, really messy, and it smells a little, too. And so she gets more allowance than me, but she doesn't do any more work than me. I don't think that's really fair.

— *Melissa, 12*

I don't really have many chores set, but I ask my mom a lot if she needs any help, but she never really asks for help, and I *want* to help sometimes. But she doesn't really let me. I think it was Sunday, my dad asked me if I could sweep the driveway, so I did that. I just have chores if my parents ask me, and I ask them sometimes.

— *Greg, 11*

I have to cook, do the windows, vacuum, I've got to take care of my little brother, I've got to take out the trash, I've got to do everything but dust. That's the only thing I don't have to do in the house.

— *Frankie, 11*

Sharing a Room

"It's kinda like enemy territory. . . ."

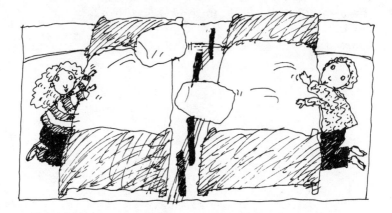

Sharing a room is a bummer. You have to put up with all the hassle when you're trying to do your homework. They just bother you, and my younger brothers come up on my bed and go, "Hi Michael. Can you come and play with me?" And I'm trying to do my homework. So I do go outside and I get yelled at, so I come back in and start doing my homework.

— *Michael, 12*

My sister and I don't share a room, but I like having my own room because you can just sit down and read and there's not much, "Amyyyyyy! Will you do this with meeee?" So I like having a room, and you can have some privacy, you know, and just sit there and think or read or do your homework.

—*Amy, 11*

I'm glad I don't share a room because my brother's room is filled with everything. I mean, he has shelves, a desk, a bureau, and a bed. I mean, he has more — a giant stereo! And none of our rooms in our house are big enough, so if we had a little sister or something, which don't, we'd have to share a room, and he's fifteen turning sixteen, which is when boys change. They really start getting really mean, and they act as if they're the boss and another parent, of course. So if I had to share a room with him, I really wouldn't. I'd probably move into the garage.

— *Carol, 11*

I share my room with my brothers and they always make big, huge messes in their area of the room, and

they never clean it up, and they always say, "Oh, this isn't my room anymore. It's yours. Only yours." And I get upset. But they always make big messes, and they make me clean it up. And they take whatever — like, if I'm in one bed, they say, "Hey, you can't stay in this bed because this is mine." And I really hate it because sometimes I have to sleep in the same bed as them, and we're all mushed together, and that's a pain.

But my brothers really just annoy me. If I have my friend up there, and then they bring their friends up, they say, "This is our room, too, so we can use the whole thing if we want to." And they start making all this racket while me and my friends are playing a game. And then maybe one of their friends will jump off the bed and land on our game and the parts will go flying all over the place. And then they say, "Oops, I'm sorry. But this is my friend's room, so I'm allowed to stay in here." And then I start yelling at them and they leave finally. And then my friends start playing in the room.

But mainly I don't use the room that often, just to go up and get my toys out of it and stuff.

— Adam, 11

My brother's younger than me, and he's always making a mess out of the room, never cleaning it up. He's taking out Matchbox cars, Legos, all these small things that get caught under the radiator, and I have to pick up most of the room. I vacuum the room, I dust the room. My parents, they both work, and they think it's only fair that I do my share of cleaning everything up, even though my brother's always making a mess with impractical stuff like Play-Doh and all kinds of small stuff that's hard to get out of places, out of the rug and everywhere.

— Wei, 11

I have a younger sister who gets scared at nighttime. We don't share a room, but at night she comes and sleeps in a sleeping bag on the floor next to me, and we talk a little bit, and then we go to sleep.

When I have friends over, because I have my own room, I can just go in and sit down and talk, and she's not coming in constantly with her friend and saying, you know, "I'm going to play in here so you have to get out." But I can go in her room sometimes because she's got a lot of toys that are mine and because she has the bigger room.

— *Bronwyn, 10*

I have to share a room with my brother, and we have bunk beds. He's a younger brother, and the problem with this guy is that he likes a messy room, and I like a clean room. So when I try to pick up the room he comes in and plays with my two younger stepbrothers. He comes in and messes up the room when he plays G.I. Joe's or whatever — or all mixed together. So I get really mad at him for that, and so Mom comes in and makes all of them clean it up, and then they don't do anything but push things under the bed. So then I *still* end up cleaning it up, which makes me kind of mad. That's the only problem.

— *Matt, 12*

I used to share a room with my sister, and it was kind of hard to have a friend over to sleep over because my little sister used to always want to get into the fun. Like, we'd be listening to the radio or dancing or something, and she'd come in and she'd try to get my friend to dance with her . . . and then she'd think she was into the act, and then she refused to leave for anything. She'd be here, like, "Now you play my dolls with me, and I'll be good." And I'm, like, "Get away from me." And it was really hard because I didn't really get any privacy at all. Now I really like my own room.

— *Jennifer, 12*

I don't share a room except for when I was young and about four when we moved into our new house, but I don't remember that. I like it better not sharing a room because you have a lot more privacy. My friends who share rooms hate it a lot because, like, if they're writing a letter, and they don't want their sister or brother to see it, they come in and they see everything. But sometimes at night, there's mice in our walls, and you get creepy, and I want my sister in my other bed because you feel better when somebody's there. But I'm glad I don't have to share a room.

— *Leah, 11*

It's nice having a room by myself 'cause then, when you have somebody in your room, it's not all crowded, and you have one bed here, one bed over there. Especially it gets crowded when you sleep with somebody, and they don't know how to sleep. They sure don't. Especially not my sister. She'll kick you one place, then kick you in another. Her feet will be in your face. One time she slept with my mother, and her feet were in my mother's mouth. It's not fun sleeping with anybody. That's why I'm glad I got my own room.

— *Nina, 11*

I share my room with my little brother, and sometimes, when I have my friends over, he always bothers me by coming in and making noises and throwing stuff at 'em. So I always kick him out. Then, when he has friends over, I go in and bother him just the same way he does to me, and then we always fight. Then we always end up making up and being brothers again.

— Harry, 13

I share a room with my sister and a lot of my friends think that's weird, but I don't really think it's that weird because I've been sharing a room with my sister since she was born — well, except when she lived in my parents' room when she was a baby. She's seven. And one of my friend's sister has her own room, but it's very small, and they have even smaller rooms than me and my sister. So I think we're pretty lucky to have a large room.

The problem with splitting up the room is my sister's

dollhouse is on my side of the room, sort of, and my dresser is right next to her bed, and we're always fighting about who should clean the rug. I always have to clean the rug because it was mine before she was born. I don't think that's fair because she's the one who makes most of the mess with her friends. They play with doll clothes and they get things all over the floor, and I have to vacuum under her bed and all that stuff, but she has to clean her bed. And she usually doesn't do that, and she has to get called in from outside to clean.

There's always a fight about who's going to clean up this part, because we share different parts of the room. It's kind of like enemy territory because she'll have shelves on her side of the room, but I'll have books in those shelves; or she'll have a coatrack on my side of the room, and the whole family's clothes are on that coatrack, and I have to share that with the whole family.

It used to be unfair because the big closet for the whole house was in my side of the room, right next to my bed. In fact, when I was little, I used to think things were coming out of there. But they never did. Except for once in one of my dreams. But sometimes I used to fantasize about having my own room in the corner, in the closet. And I used to make little rooms with my quilt, and I'd make a little room, and I'd clear out all the clothes, and my mom would get angry.

— *Jason, 11*

I used to share a room with my older sister and she used to be, like, really neat, and I used to have my clothes all around and all my toys all around, and she'd yell at me, and I hated it because I couldn't help it. I was only little.

— *Lydia, 11*

I share a room with my older brother and my second youngest brother. It's crowded because my older brother works on third shift, and he's not home at night, so one of us either sleeps on the couch or in the bedroom. Well, me and my brother really switch on and off so it's pretty hard. My older brother uses the table for his clothes, and I use the dresser and my other brother uses the floor for clothes.

— Daryl, 13

You don't get much privacy. My sister, when you try to get to sleep, she just talks the whole night, even when she's asleep! She says, "Courtney, what you going to do in the morning? How are you going to get dressed? What are you wearing tomorrow? What are you going to do tomorrow?" And everything. So, I say, "Christie, shut up." You know, she really bugs me.

— Courtney, 10

I don't like sharing a room because my baby sister, sometimes when she's asleep, has nightmares. She yells right in my ear because she sleeps in the next bed next to me.

It's kind of disgusting because I'm older than her, and if I have a friend over, we're talking private talk, and she likes to go in and hear everything, and when I'm done she goes and tells my father. So it's no fun sharing a room.

— Teodolinda, 13

What I hate about sharing a room is I share a room with my younger sister. We put our beds together at night because she's scared to sleep by herself, and when we put our beds together she can't sleep. She punches me in the stomach sleeping, and she doesn't know it, though. She slaps me in the face, and when I want to hit her I can't because she's sleeping. So that's what I hate about sharing a room with my sister.

And, also, when I buy a poster she says she doesn't like prints, or she doesn't like my poster and she doesn't

want that poster. She just wants to put up Peanuts post-
ers and stuff. And I *hate* that.

— Rudi, 12

Once my mother moved into a new apartment, and I
had to share a bedroom with my brother, and we had
to share the same bed. So once, in the morning, I put
my coat on the top of the bed and he comes and throws
it on the ground. My sweater and everything, he comes
and throws that on the floor, too. So at night, when we
went to bed, it was around twelve midnight, I came and
pushed him off the bed. All he wanted to do was get
back at me, so he got up and took my shoes and went
into the sink and filled them up with water. When I got
up in the morning I put my shoes on and all my shoes
were all wet. I just felt like punching him hard.

— Bernard, 13

One thing I hate about sharing a room with my little
brother is when sometimes he might use the bathroom
on the bed. I have to get up, take the blankets off, put
on new ones, go with him to the bathroom, change his
pants, and come back. I never get to sleep. That's why
sometimes I come to school late.

— Noel, 13

I used to share my room. My older brother slept in it
with me. I don't know how he did it, but one day he
started rolling around or something in his sleep, and
now he rolls around every single night. And, you know,
it used to bug me. I used to call, "Ma, he's rolling around
again, he's bugging me." My mother would come up and
say, "You stop rolling around." It would take him awhile,
and then he'd start rolling around again.

Besides the fact I like to keep my stuff to my own,
and he likes to keep his stuff to his own, but each of us
goes on the other person's side of the room. So my

mother, after a while, put up a big wall in the middle of the room. Well, it wasn't permanent. It was just a piece of board and stuff. And then, you know, my brother had his own privacy, and I had my own privacy, and now I have my own room. But my sister is going to be born and gets my brother's old room, and my brother's moving in with me again. And it's going to be even worse.

— *BJ, 13*

Special Times

"It's a special time when we don't have a lot of fights."

I was going to a spelling bee. My brother is kind of like a bully, so I never expected him to say anything to me. When I walked out the door on the way to go to the spelling bee, he said, "I wish you luck. I wish you to win." That made me feel good because he never hardly listens to what I have to say.

— *Rudi, 12*

When my sister does something good for me, she usually remembers it, so that later she'll say, "Well, I did all this for you, and you've never done anything for me." But usually I don't keep a record of the stuff I do for her, so I really don't have anything to say back. So the good times usually end up in fights.

— *Todd, 12*

I like cooking with my older sister because we just both like to cook — and when my mom's not home, if we're in a good mood, we cook together. It's fun.

— *Rebecca, 10*

See, it's sort of a special time when we don't have a lot of fights. We don't have them constantly, but you know, we have them a lot, sort of. And once we went to the beach, and Martin, my older brother, let me get up on his shoulders. Then we'd walk out in the water, and he'd let me drop. So that was sort of fun — it was a special time, because we didn't have any arguments or anything.

— *Randy, 12*

We went on vacation to Colorado last summer for two weeks. My older brother was really nice to me and we went hiking off into the mountains. We were a couple miles from the car when this big thunderstorm started, and it started hailing . . . he was really nice to me then because I was scared and everything.

— *Jennifer, 10*

This was in Pittsburgh. We went to a park one day, okay? And everybody there was having a baseball game. I was seven years old. My brother was, I think, ten. And all the ten-year-olds and eleven- and twelve-year-olds were having this gigantic baseball game. And nobody would let me play. My brother was one of the best in the whole thing. And he said, "Okay, if you're not going to let my brother play, I'm not going to play." And that's one of the only times he's really done that. And then they let me play. I had the best time there. I mean it. It was so fun.

— *Tim, 10*

Often my sister does this: When she's going to the movies — sometimes she doesn't — but a lot of times she'll talk her friends into letting me go with her. I don't sit with them, but she talks them into letting me go.

— *John, 11*

One time Wally was off somewhere, I don't know where he was. He's a neighbor of mine. And so there was nobody home to play with. So I was just walking around outside. And my sister and her two friends were playing. So I walked over there, and I was desperate. And I said, "Can I play?" Everybody except my sister said no. And my sister said, "If you won't let him play, then you can't stay here." So I just started playing. We were playing with the cats so it wasn't that bad.

— *Ben, 11*

I went for a trip during school to Bermuda. And my sister Lauren, well, we were having a real fun time because she would drive the motorbike, and I would sit

behind, and it was really fun because she would always make these turns, and we'd always go fast. And we'd make fun of my parents because they'd go less than the speed limit, and they'd just chug there. We'd use these funny little beeps on them. We had so much fun with that.

— *Layne, 11*

One special thing that I remember about me and my brother when we were little kids, we were in the house one day, and my mother was in the bedroom with my father, and me and my brother got in the medicine cabinet, right? And my brother put all this makeup on his face while we were mixing stuff in the kitchen, and we melted one of my mother's bowls trying to cook in it. And my mother came out of the bedroom, and she was mad.

— *Tanya, 12*

Whenever sometimes my parents will be yelling at us, like, "You ungrateful kids!" and then they leave, me and my younger brother start making faces and talking about them and how we feel. And it just sort of makes me feel

better that I can talk about it with someone that understands. So it just makes us closer in a way, sometimes.

— *Danielle, 12*

Last year I went to Florida with my brother. We flew
on the plane by ourselves, and we met people down
there. He was really fun to be with because he was just
as excited as I was. We really enjoyed pointing out different things to each other and showing each other where
we'd been and what parts we liked most, and we really
got along really well.

— *Julie, 12*

Right before Christmastime me and my older brother
wrap up things that we have in pieces of paper and tape
them and give them to each other. We trade things. It's
neat to get stuff that you don't know that you're going
to get. And they aren't presents that people go out and
buy. They're stuff that the person already has.

— *Leslie, 11*

I have three brothers and sisters and we don't do anything fun together.

— *Kari, 11*

Sometimes it's not bad to have a little brother going around with you in the malls to look at all the stuff that you like instead of your parents going, "Oh, it's too expensive, it's too expensive." They complain. So sometimes I think it's really neat to have a little brother. I don't know if I'd like to *be* a little brother, though.

— *Wei, 11*

I have a younger sister, and sometimes we'll go outside and jump on our now-broken trampoline, or swing on a swing or play with our dog. We just have fun together, and we hug and stuff. We get mad at each other, but we always make up.

— *Bronwyn, 10*

My older sister is going to be going to college. She's seventeen. For me it's going to be kind of lonesome because almost all the time she's in the house, or when I feel bad, she just cheers me up lots of times. Also, lots of times she helps me with my schoolwork and tells me what teachers look for. Also, I'm going to have a lot more housework to do, since she's gone. But fortunately we won't miss her that much because the college that she's going to, she'll be able to come back about every other weekend or more often.

— *Eli, 13*

My brother, the things he finds special with me are, like, taking me to parties. He'll say, "Oh, I'm taking Craig to the dentist's office," or something like that. And my mother will go, "Oh, fine!" And he'll take me to a party or something.

— *Craig, 14*

We have this summer house up in New Hampshire, and we just bought twenty more acres up there. And the two of us, we have a big huge rock up there, my younger sister and I. We go up on the rock and we have parties and stuff like that. We bring our lunch up there sometimes. And we don't let our parents up there either.

— *Sophie, 13*

When we're with company or people we don't like, then we're really good friends. And, you know, we always whisper to each other about the other people when they're not looking, and it's fun.

— *Melissa, 12*

Sometimes when my sister's having trouble with her homework I help her with that. And sometimes when she's warming up to pitch in a baseball game I sometimes (because I'm a catcher) get down and catch for her until she's warmed up.

— *Terry, 12*

I like going fishing with my brother because we usually go down, and we rent a boat, we go out on the river, we fish for a few hours, then we go home and have lunch. Then we go back down, and we get a thing that holds the fish and tells how heavy it is. We always have a contest to see who catches the bigger fish.

— *Matt, 13*

Sometimes I can't go to sleep and my older brother will come in my bed and we'll turn on the TV. We're really not supposed to do that because my parents and everybody's sleeping. But we like to sneak a lot of things, like at night, if we're both hungry, we'll go downstairs, and we'll get into the refrigerator or something.

— *Deidra, 11*

I have a younger sister, and we have this little mailbox thing. She has a big oatmeal round box thing that she

taped on our door. And I have this bag I stenciled on, and I put it on my door handle, and my mom has this hot chocolate coffee box she stuck on her door. And at nighttime sometimes we'll put little notes into our boxes and read them before we go to bed and stuff.

— *Bronwyn, 10*

The closest I felt with my brother was when my father died. He was there when I needed him. And you know, every time I started to cry he said, "It'll be all right." And that's really the reason. That's it. That's when I was closest.

—*Anne, 12*

Jealousy

"She thinks Mom loves me better, I think Mom loves her better."

My brothers are jealous of me because I'm the youngest of thirteen people, and I get more presents at Christmas and stuff.

— *Vincent, 13*

I'm kind of jealous, but I understand why. You know, there are certain things I know I can't do, but I'm still jealous about them. My older brother can, like, go out late and invite his friends over late at night when I'm asleep, and he can stay up a lot later. Lots of times I like to watch these shows or specials on later but I have to go to bed early, and I get up later than he does. He gets to go to bed later, and he still gets up earlier. My parents just say he's older. I don't see the difference, really. When you sleep, you sleep. I mean you need to rest. That's it.

— *Carol, 11*

My brothers and sisters are always jealous of me because whenever I have a lot of money I'll go out and buy something really nice, like a graphite fly rod. My little sister got real jealous, but she doesn't like fishing. But she does like to have something around so she can say, "Look what I have!" She finally gave up trying to buy things off me. Sometimes I get jealous of my sister who has these little things, and then she tries giving auctions and things like that. She'll go up into my room and say, "Okay, this is two dollars, two dollars. Do I see three dollars, three dollars, three dollars, three dollars?" And so sometimes she goes for ridiculous prices, like a teeny little rubber ball for two dollars. And you know, they're worth about two cents.

Sometimes I buy from her, and sometimes I'm thinking about buying and she gives up on me and she just says, "Here, I don't need it." Sometimes my mom will

come in and say, "Listen, if you don't need it, just give it to David."

My younger brother also gets jealous. He likes having money. He's just learned that pennies are not worth much. They weigh a lot, but they're not worth much, so he's getting better at spying and stealing.

So I keep finding out he's rich when I'm poor; when I was rich the day before. He keeps trying to steal my money, and sometimes he walks into my room and dumps the money out on my desk. Sometimes when he steals, though, he'll leave a mess, and I'll go around and find my desk drawers out of place, and I'll find my desk drawer on top of my bed. It's pretty obvious. I go into his room and say, "Julien, give me my money." And he'll say, "Oh, I didn't take any money, I didn't take any money." And I say, "Julien, what's in your fist?" And he goes, "No, no, no!" and he runs around the house. Eventually I'll find out what's in there.

He's getting into the phase where he's getting rid of his pennies. He has about thirty pounds of pennies in this little box, and once I had a twenty dollar bill hidden in my desk and when I walked back, I couldn't find it. Where's all my money? But I looked right back where I had hidden it, and I found about two pounds of pennies lying there. He leaves his little calling cards wherever he goes. He figures they're worth the same. He thinks, "I just want one piece instead of all these." But really, he leaves me forty cents, and he gets twenty dollars.

— *David, 11*

Sometimes my little sister and big sister always agree on stuff and, like, one time when I was with my dad, they both wanted to go to some girlie store to get all these bracelets and stuff, and I think I wanted to go to the aquarium or something.

— *Michael, 11*

I'm jealous of my older brother a lot because he's got a job and he's got a lot of friends in the high school.

He's got a really good reputation around the place. He's like a police officer when my parents aren't home because he always tells us what to do, you know, like he's in charge. I wish I could do that, but he won't let me do that to my younger brother so I'm really jealous of him when he does that.

— *Matthew, 12*

I get jealous of my younger brother sometimes because sometimes he plays tricks on my mother. He might say to her, for example, "They're outside playing baseball, and I'm not getting to," but five minutes ago he might have said, "Well it's okay. I don't want to play outside." He tries to get people to feel sorry for him, and then it makes me jealous because my mother pays more attention to him than to me.

— *Emily, 12*

The biggest time I was jealous — and I still am — was when my father taught my brother how to use his hatchet when he was eleven. I still haven't learned how to use it, and I'm already eleven, so I'm still waiting to learn how to use the hatchet. Something tells me I never will because my father lives in an apartment, and there isn't much to cut down in our apartment.

— *Daniel, 11*

One of my brothers ran away because of all the attention I was getting. He just went next door at his friend's house. He came home the next day and said, "I'm getting sick and tired of this, Dad. May I please get more of the attention?" And I'm, like, "No you may not. So, nah! Get out of here!" I was really mean. I was mean when I was young.

— *Sharon, 11*

I get jealous sometimes because my brother and my sisters are younger than me, and one of my sisters likes

to be treated like a baby. When my mother says something to her, she always says my sister's name and says
"honey" after it. I'd like to have that said to me, not that
it's a baby word. My mom always calls me "Jule" instead
of saying like she says my sister's name, like, "Beth,
honey."

— *Julie, 12*

One time, my father bought this new shirt, and I liked
it, too. He said, "Do you want one of these shirts? I can
go pick you one up at work tomorrow." I said, "Yeah."
So the next day he came home with these pajamas for
my sister and shoes and everything. I mean, he didn't
have anything for me. Then I got mad.

— *Melody, 12*

There is a lot of jealousy between me and my older
sister because she thinks that Mom loves me better, and
I think that Mom loves her better. Last week my sister
went to San Francisco, and next week she's going to
Europe, and I haven't gone anywhere this year, and so
I think it's really unfair. But my mom keeps saying,
"Well, she's older, Kari, she's older," but I'm a lot nicer
to my mother, and my sister's a lot meaner. But I never
get anything, and she always gets everything. She gets
to go a lot of places where I never get to go. It really
doesn't make a difference about my age, but my mom
always says, "But she's older."

— *Kari, 11*

I'm most of the time jealous of my older brother because he's so popular with all the kids my age, and some
of the kids he *doesn't even know, know him.* Then some
of the kids he knows know me, but it's not like the kids
that know him, because, like, all the people that know
me, I know. But he doesn't know half the people that
know him, and they think he's so great.

— *Leslie, 11*

My younger brother is jealous more of me than I am of him. He's mostly jealous of me when I pour some milk. He goes, "Do you have more than me?" and he goes and takes some more milk. I just let it go. And then sometimes for dessert, I'll take, like, three cookies and joke about having four. So he goes, "Oh, you have four, so I got to take four, too." So he ends up taking four. I let it go. Sometimes I'm jealous. He's only nine, and he gets these nifty little things, and I try to use them, and he goes, "No, you can't use them." So then I reverse it. When he wants to use something of mine, I'll just say he can't use it, and he'll tell my mother, and I'll have to share or else *I* can't use it.

— *Michael, 12*

My younger sister and I are on a swim team. Since she's in a younger group, she's really good. She made it to some really high rankings. She's one of the best in the state, and I was only, like, fourteenth or so. She walks home with a whole bunch of gold medals and lots of first ribbons, and it really kind of makes me jealous, but I think my sister's jealous of me because I get to use the stove and other little things. I'm put in charge in babysitting and things like that so it works out both ways.

— *Amy, 11*

My younger sister's jealous of me because she knows I'm sixteen months older than her, and my twelfth birthday's coming up, and so I get a ten-speed. I get a lot more things earlier than she does. She's jealous of me because she knows I get better grades than she does because she has a hard time in school. But then I'm sort of jealous of her because she has better looks and stuff. She can wear all these styles that are really fashionable now, like designer jeans and all this stuff, and they just don't fit me right, but she's not fat, and she's not skinny, she's just regular. But she also knows that since I'm on the town swim team, that I can swim better than she does because I worked hard at it. She also has trouble in that. We have a summer cottage on a lake, and so she worked really hard on her swimming. When I do other things in the water, it sort of makes her mad because she cannot do good dives and stuff like that.

— *Leah, 11*

My fourteen-year-old brother just got a new job, and he's getting his paycheck. He's always flaunting his money around, and that makes me and my two younger brothers kind of jealous of his money.

— *Allison, 12*

I always get jealous of my older sister because she gets some designer jeans. I tell my mother to get me some and she goes, "No. . . . Why don't you go and ask your father for some money?" It gets me real mad, and

I get so jealous that tears start coming out of my eyes. My mother's got the two little ones spoiled rotten, and it gets me real mad because the two oldest ones, they get at least three dollars a week, and the two little ones get anything they want. I feel so left out because I'm in the middle, and I don't get anything. It's real annoying.

— Marisol, 13

The real jealousy problem is that I live with my father, and my brother lives with my mother. He really would rather live with my father than my mother. He's sort of jealous because he wants to live where I'm living.

— Claudia, 13

I'm the middle one in the household. I'm always jealous of my sister because everybody says she's prettier than me, that she's got more body than me, and that she knows more people than me and everything. I'm jealous of her because she's got more boyfriends, and a lot of people say she's nicer, and they talk about her a lot. People ask me, "Where's Betty? Where's Betty?" And I get jealous of her because she knows a lot of people and I don't. My brother gets jealous over us because we get anything — not anything, because my sister gets mostly everything. I'm maybe jealous of my sister because she always gets anything, and she's pretty. She's got a lot of connections, and she's got a lot of boyfriends. She plays with all the boys. She says that she has no more boyfriends but she's got a lot.

— Sandra, 13

I get real jealous of my younger sister because my father's wife likes my sister a bit more because she's more organized than I am. I have a really messy room. My sister is really neat, and so she's nicer to my sister.

When my stepmother gets in a bad mood, she blames it on me instead of my sister.

— *Ellen, 13*

Sometimes I get jealous because my sister sometimes gets most of the attention because she usually tries to act cute to my mother (she's older, she's sixteen years old), and she *always* tries to act cute. She's getting a driver's permit so she's getting a lot of attention from my dad to help her for driving. Sometimes I'm just in my room doing reports for school, and she'd just be romping around the whole house being cute to everybody. My mother and father usually pay a lot of attention to her when I'm off in my room alone.

— *Mark, 13*

Well, one thing is my mother thinks that my younger brother is too skinny, and I really think he is, too. When we're, like — say we're at a carnival — my mom, she would buy him popcorn *and* ice cream, and I would just get an ice cream. I don't think that's fair just because she thinks he's skinny.

— *Lucy, 11*

The jealousy usually comes because both my sister and I get involved in a lot of activities. One sister feels that she's being cheated out of an opportunity that the other sister is getting. A lot of times my younger sister gets to do a lot of things that I had to wait to do 'til I was older, and there's sort of a feeling of anger in that. She began to take tennis lessons earlier, and she got to start an instrument earlier and go to overnight camp earlier, for example. Some of the experiences that she's having at a younger age make me angry because I feel that my parents sort of neglected to see that I wanted that sort of thing when I was her age. Sometimes it's my parents going to things like her games. They go to all my sister's softball games, but they never came to any of my basketball games here at school. I often sort of felt cheated about that. But also I'm sort of glad they didn't come other times. My performance wasn't too good. I'm sort of the old standby the coach puts in at the last minute.

— *Kate, 12*

Tattling

"My brother's favorite hobby is to tattletale on me."

My brother is older than me, and he never tattletales on me, but I *always* tattletale on him because I like to get him in trouble. My parents always believe me, even if it's not all the way true.

— *Nadine, 10*

My fourteen-year-old brother always tattletales on me. Whenever it's really important, a matter of life or death, and my parents are not supposed to know, my brother always tells. He always manages a way, even if it's not really bad, to make it sound bad, just to get me in trouble. He *loves* doing that. It's like his favorite thing to tattletale on me. He always used to do it a lot when I was little. And whenever I wanted to tattletale on him he always used to, like, threaten me, like he was going to beat me up or something.

— *Kim, 12*

My little brother's favorite hobby is to tattletale on me. He always does it, no matter what the situation. If I break something, he'll tell. If I'm going to get something for my mother for her birthday, he'll tell. Everything he tells. And one time I went down to my friend's house — we were making a surprise for my little brother — and he told my mom that we were making a surprise for him, and we got in trouble because the surprise wasn't very nice.

— *Matt, 13*

I'm the one who tattletales, because sometimes my big brother really keeps on calling me names, and he does all this mean stuff. He takes things out of my room without asking, and it really annoys me, so I just say, "Mom, tell him to leave me alone." My mother just comes and says, "Charlie, leave her alone." But he just keeps on doing it. He doesn't listen. Of course, big brothers would do that.

— *Carol, 11*

My older brothers like to beat up on me. And no matter what, they never get in trouble because they're larger than my mother. So when I tell, they just say, "Stop it," and they keep doing it. Where, with my sister, she lies about me to get me in trouble because I tell on her a lot. And so she lies when I didn't do anything, and then she says, "Oh no, I didn't do that." And since she's older than me, my mother believes her, and I always get in trouble.

— *Kari, 11*

I have a younger brother. He isn't really that great in keeping secrets or anything. Sometimes, like, if I get frustrated with him when I'm babysitting him at home, you know, maybe I'll give him a little shove or something. But when my mom and dad come home, he'll tell right away just because I got so frustrated with him. Or, if I do something I'm not supposed to, like, if I go down to a store (if I have some extra lunch money) and buy, you know, some candy or something, my brother will always tell on me. He'll say, "Oh, oh, Wei bought something, Wei bought something and he's not supposed to buy that!"

And, well, it works both ways: I have to say that I tell too. You know, I'm not this super angel who doesn't tell at all about my brother, but he's not too terrific himself. He's always telling about me. He's telling my parents a lot of lies, too. Well, you know, not bad lies, but sometimes they turn a little out of hand. Like, "He punched me, and I got a bloody nose," or something like that. And I don't usually punch him that hard. You know, if I punch him it's moderate, not a real giant punch or anything.

— *Wei, 11*

One time, I was fooling around and I had a little fire in the garage. And, you know, I cleaned it up and stuff, and my brother said he wouldn't tell on me. But it turns out he did. My mother asked me, "Well, what'd you light the fire for?" And I said I had nothing better to do. So she said not to worry about it, and she just didn't want it to ever happen again. And, well, at the time I was already in trouble about something else.

— *BJ, 13*

One time I had candy in my room and I wasn't supposed to because it was ant season, and we had ants.

And my little sister found it. She used to share a room with me. And my mom got wicked mad at me because I had candy in my room.

— *Jennifer, 12*

One time, my brother (he was about eight years old) rode into town on his bike, and he wasn't supposed to ride in. So, you know, I told on him. I had nothing better to do. And then he got mad at me. And, well, actually before, he was trying to bribe me not to. And he does that regularly, you know? And that didn't work — well, it worked for a while, but then it didn't. You know, I got mad at him and so I told on him. And he got in trouble. He got sent to his room for a while, and I felt a little guilty, but I guess he needed it.

— *BJ, 13*

One time I had just gotten a new radio; an AM-FM cassette player for my birthday. And I told my brother and my stepcousins and everybody that I didn't want anybody to touch it. And so my brother came in my room — my younger brother — and he said he needed some D-cell batteries for his — I think it was his G.I. Joe tank or something like that. And so anyway, he took one battery, and when I came home I didn't know it was him. I discovered it because the antenna had been un-hooked, and it had been unplugged. So I opened it up, and I found that a battery was missing, and I went and told my mom. And then she asked Ben, and Ben goes, "No!" before she's finished. So then I asked him privately in our room, and I said I wouldn't do anything to him, but I did. When he told me the truth, I told on him and he got in trouble. He got yelled at.

— *Matt, 12*

My sister tattletales on me and I tattletale on her. But my parents don't really believe us because we fight all the time and, I mean, we just tattletale, like, if she'll kick me, and I'll kick her. We'll tear each other up, and we'll tell.

— Leah, 11

I have a little brother, and when he does something, he says, "Well, I didn't do it," and that someone else did it, usually my little sister, who's younger than him, and she doesn't even know what he's talking about because she's only one.

— Heather, 10

My younger sister never tattletales on me, and I don't tattletale on her. And if we get in trouble, it's probably because my parents hear us because we've got a small house.

— Amy, 11

One time I went outside when I'm not supposed to, right? And when I came back in the house, my sister said, "I'm going to tell Ma." And I said, "Don't tell," right? And I said, "I'll give you anything you want," right? And she said, "Give me a dollar." Right? So I gave her a dollar. And then, when my mother came home, she told.

— Erica, 13

My father and mother won't let me go anywhere. So once I went to this other school I used to go to. They didn't know. They thought I went to the grocery store. Then, when my brother saw me coming from there I said, "Don't tell. *Please.* I'll let you have anything you want." Then he said, "Let me use your radio for a month." I said, "No way!" Then he ran back home. I caught him because he can't run fast. I told him, "Okay, okay." Then, when he went home, he didn't know that my radio was broke. Then he went to use it, it was broke. Then he went to tell my father.

— Felicia, 11

Like, when I clean up the room sometimes, I look around to see if nobody's looking, I look down the hall and sweep the trash under the bed, and then, my little brother, he'll be peeking in the closet, and so he sees me and tells.

— Brad, 12

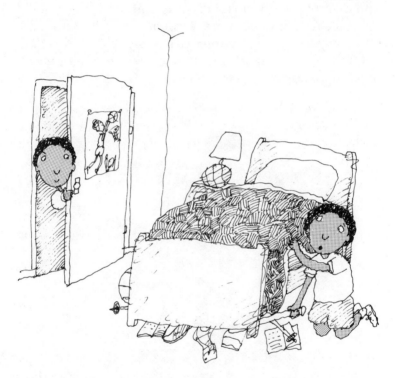

My sister and my brother always tell on me. Yesterday I was talking on the phone with a boy, and my sister told my mother, and I didn't get punished. My mother just said, "I want you to get phone calls." But she didn't want phone calls after 10:00. And my sister told my father. My brother always tells on me that I'm calling boys, or that I'm doing crank calls, and that I always argue on the phone.

I tell on my sister and my brother. When she talks to her boyfriend, I tell my mother everything she says to

him and everything he says to her — I always pick up
the other line.

— Sandra, 13

My older sister just got this new rabbit and the rabbit's
sort of sick, or she thinks it's sick. And I suggested that
he might have this awful disease. And she goes, "Robin,
if you say that once more, I'm going to tell Mom, and
you're going to have to apologize to my rabbit." And I'm,
"I don't believe this!" And so she told my mom, and I
had to apologize to her rabbit.

— Robin, 12

My sister is *always* telling on me. I'd rather not tell
on her. I'd rather just fight her. But, like, if I do something I'm not supposed to, even if it isn't to her directly,
she'll go, "Mommy, Sophie did this and that." And I
always get punished.

— Sophie, 13

When we're in my room together, we make sure we find something so we can say, "I saw you do that, and if you don't do something for me, then I'll tell." Or something like that. And my brother can always find something for me because we're always doing something wrong. We always do things wrong because we're not perfect at all. As a matter of fact, we're bad-prone. We're the worst things in the world, to put it to you in a sentence. I don't know. We're prone to being bad — it's got to come. We have to do something wrong at least once a day.

— *Craig, 14*

My sister and I don't do too many bad things. We don't really tattle on each other. We sort of cover each other. Like, we protect each other. Because if I tell on her, she'll tell on me, and vice versa. So the majority of the time we both don't tattle on each other. Lots of times, though, she tries to take advantage. Like, when my dad is away for a couple of days or something, she says, "If you let me have boys over to the house, I'll let you have girls over to the house," and it doesn't exactly work, because I don't really have girls over to the house. And she always tries to give me the short end of the stick. She's seventeen.

— *Eli, 13*

My big brother, he has a lot of secrets and stuff. *A lot.* Some of them I can't even tell here, well, not in this book. They're always bad — well, some of them are bad — and I can't tell my mom or anything. And so I always threaten to tell my mom and never do because, see, I know what he'd think of me if I ever did. I don't really care what he thinks of me, but I just don't want to tattle. Never.

— *Jason, 11*

Sometimes my little brother wants to use something that I'm using. I say no. And so he goes into one of these states of sudden shock, and then he starts crying. And so he takes a swing at me. Sometimes if he hits you, then you hit him back, and then you don't tell because you're older or something. You always figure, "Well I'm not going to tell because that's babyish," or something like that. But then he goes and tells because you hit him after he had hit you.

— *Jonathan, 11*

One time I was putting some wood in the wood stove because we heat one of the rooms in our house with a wood stove. The lid dropped on the rug, and it made this big mark, and my sister goes and tells. I was just about to tell, and it really bothers me. My mom was on the phone, but as soon as she got off, I was just going to tell my mom what I did. My sister bugs me a lot.

—*Abe, 11*

I've said some pretty rotten things, but I've never tattled on anybody. And I've never been tattled on either.

— *Jordan, 11*

Like, if my parents ask me to babysit, and I say, "No," and they say, "Why," and I go, "Well, because my brothers are jerks." Well, Kenny's my oldest middle brother. He's a jerk, and they'll go, "Well, why don't you ever tell us about it?" Because, like, if my brothers get in trouble for something because I tell on them because they're probably doing something bad, then I feel sad for them, so I don't always tell on them, and I wish I had told on them later.

— *Heather, 12*

I have two people in my family that tattletale: My older sister and my older brother. Okay. My sister, she tattletales on everything I ever tell her. I tell her secrets, and she goes back and tells my mother everything. And my brother, he likes to spy on me and tell my mother things.

— *Dora, 12*

I don't have any brothers or sisters, *but* if I had a younger brother or sister they'd probably read my diary and say, "She likes so and so and she likes this and she likes that." And then they would probably get punished, and then they would get off scot-free, and they'd go around and blab to the whole neighborhood: "Patricia likes this, Patricia likes that."

— *Patricia, 12*

My little brother just recently was told that he could not have anything until dinner. He took one of the little chocolate puddings into his room and he hid it under his sweatshirt. And I was there. He must have thought I was very stupid. He turned his head around suspiciously, and I went into his room and I said, "What's the spoon for?" And he said, "I'm just building something with it." And I said, "Well, Jonathan, what's this?" And I tapped on his sweatshirt, and there was this little box under there, and I took it out, and I said, "You know you're not supposed to eat this before dinner," and he said, "Well, I wasn't going to eat it." And I said, "What were you going to do with it?" And he said, "Well I was building something with it." And I said, "Jonathan, if you tell me the truth I won't tell Mommy." And he said, "Well, Emily, that's the truth." And he started crying. And I said, "Jonathan, tell me the truth." And he said, "Okay. I was lying. I was not going to build anything with it. I was going to eat it. I was hungry, and all I get to have before dinner is fruit." And he was like yelling at me. And I ended up telling my mother, but didn't tell him that I told her.

— Emily, 12

One night my brother brought home a friend — and this was a girlfriend. My older brother — actually both of them are older, but it was Vinnie — who brought home his girlfriend — he told me not to tell because he was going to get in trouble. And I was like, "Oh, no, I gotta tell. I gotta tell." But I didn't. Not until a year later. But he still yelled at me. She — *eeei, yiii, yiii* — she ended up sleeping over. In my bed. My brother was sleeping in his own bed.

— Sharon, 11

To have a good time with my younger sisters, you have to do everything good. If you do something bad, they will definitely go and tattle on you. They will tattle on you and you will get in so much trouble. And if they ask for a drink of water you have to run up and get one or they'll go and tell about that. They're just pains.

— *Victoria, 12*

I feel that tattling is a form of revenge. My sister and I, we often tattle on each other because it's a way of getting back at a sister or brother because you are angry, and it's sort of a form of warfare and feuds. And what I would say is not to tattle, but to keep it to yourselves, and work it out yourselves.

— *Kate, 12*

Secrets and Pretending

"When we're spying on our parents we have secret signs."

Me and my brother have a special code. And we were showing it to my mom and asked her if she knew what it was. She said she couldn't figure it out. And we said, "Good." Because then we could pass secret notes. When we're spying on our parents in the windows, we have all these secret signs. Like, we make a bird call, and that means to go somewhere; and we move our hands in some way that makes a sign. It's just that so we know what we're talking about. And our parents don't really know about that. So it's pretty secret.

— *Leslie, 11*

Me and my younger sister like to play that we're grown up and married. We cook and we use beads and papers and stuff, like, for rice.

My younger sister, she has dolls, and she pretends that those are her kids, and she's feeding them.

— *Rudi, 12*

Sometimes we set up little clubs, but they never worked for any long period of time because it was kind of silly. It wouldn't have worked because it wasn't set up right. We'd start something, but then we'd get in a fight, and it wouldn't work out. And we couldn't start anything like a long game. We knew it wouldn't finish because someone would call the other person a cheater, and it would just all fall through.

— *Paul, 12*

This is my young brother Kevin, he's two. If he doesn't want to play with some of his toys, we play Popeye. So we'll be playing Popeye, and I say, "All right, it's time to

eat your spinach. We gotta get some muscles so we can go beat Bruno" — that's my brother Elliot. And Elliot says, "Popeye, I'm gonna beat you up." So then my big brother eats his spinach and then he goes to beat Kevin up. But then I say, "You gotta eat some more spinach," and he eats his spinach all up.

— Tanya, 12

Once, when I came in real late one night, and my brother asked me where I was, I said, "I just saw a spaceship out there." And he goes, "No sir." And I go, "Yes sir. And the door was open and I went in and saw a space creature. He was green, and he had things growing out of his head." And then my brother believed me. And he goes, "No sir. You didn't really see a spaceship." And I says, "Yes sir. It had, like, these colored light bulbs on it." And I drew a picture, so he could believe me, of a spaceship. And he goes, "No you didn't, because there'd be marks on the ground or something." And I go, "Come outside," because there was, like, construction work being done on the buildings, and he goes, "No, that was just from the construction people." I go, "No sir. There was a real, live spaceship out here." He goes, "No way!" And I go, "Okay. You're right." And he goes, "I knew it wasn't out here!"

— Theo, 12

Once me and my whole family went to the lake. Me and my brother were pretending we were cops and he said, "There goes a robber." And I said, "No there doesn't. I don't see anybody." Then he said, "We're playing pretending, aren't we?" And I said, "Oh, yeah."

I jumped in the lake, then he jumped in after me. And he got caught in the sand. "Bernie, Bernie, there's somebody grabbing my leg." And I said, "No there isn't. Come on. Hurry up! Are we playing or not?" And he said, "No, I'm serious, I'm serious!" And I said, "No there isn't." And I went over there, and I went towards him, and I said, "Come on!" and I grabbed his arm, and I pulled him, and we kept going swimming. Then something else caught me, and I said, "Now *my* leg is caught!" And he said, "No it isn't. Come on, we're still pretending." And I said, "Aw, there's a shark eating my leg!" And he said, "Come on, man, let's stop playing around!" And I said, "But there really is, there really is!" And we had this kind of liquid that was, like, fake blood. So I put my leg up, I put the fake blood on, and I said, "See? I'm caught, I'm caught." He came towards me, and he grabbed me, and he ran out, and I said, "Aha, fake blood." So, we all just play around like that.

— *Bernard, 13*

Sometimes my brother wants to play G.I. Joe because he gets little water guns — that's what he buys with his extra money if he ever gets any. And then if I don't play like he wants, he goes, "You're not doing it right. You have to pretend different." And sometimes I don't *want* to do it that way. Sometimes he says, "If I shoot you, you have to die until I wake you up." Sometimes I end up sitting there for, like, a half an hour because he just sits there giggling at me, and it really bugs me some-times.

— *Jonathan, 11*

hee hee hee hee

Me and my younger sister, we have a pool. We have a rope swing that we put down, and we try to pretend we're, like, hairy people. We sometimes hook the rope in a loop, so you can put your foot in it. Then we swing out across and we try not to bump into anything, and we try not to let anything touch the water. Otherwise the alligator monster gets us or something. Then we have to try to pull each other out without the alligator monster getting you. And you can't use the rope. Each time the rope gets shorter and shorter. And then we have to survive some other way and get across the pool some other way, without touching.

— *Nicole, 11*

Last year when I was ten I pretended with my brother that I was playing spaceship. I was in a train, like a train that can go into space around to the planets. I was the one that drives the train, and my brother was on the back of the train saying, "All aboard." I said, "Ready to take off." Then I said, "Ten, nine, eight, seven, six . . . then take off! We're in space now. Over." Like that. Then he said, "All right, where are we going this time?" I said, "We're going to some planet, an alien planet." He said, "Where's that?" I said, "I don't know. Let's go around to the black hole." My brother said, "Nooo, we'll be sucked in." Then I said, "Then where are we going to go?" Then my brother said, "Somewhere, I don't know." My mother told me, "Dinner!" So we went to dinner.

— *Tommy, 11*

Stepsisters and Stepbrothers

". . . It means more people to play with."

I like having stepbrothers and sisters because it means more people to play with, like, for tag, games after dinner, and things of that sort. And it's kind of nice. It's fun if we make up a new game. We have one called chase, and there's two teams, and one team chases the other team around at night in the dark.

— Matt, 12

Sometimes it's different because my stepsibs try to act like they're directly related to me. My parents sometimes do stuff for them that they wouldn't do for me. My stepbrother and sister, they get to do everything. There's more pressure on me because I'm directly related to my father, and he's getting married to this other woman, and they're her two children. I'm not always with my father because he lives in Maine, and every time I go up there I expect there to be more pressure on my stepbrother and sister because they're always with my father, but there's more pressure on me to be friends with them and do stuff with them. I guess it's because they're younger. But it's weird.

— *Seth, 12*

Both my parents are remarried, and I've got eleven stepbrothers and sisters. It's really a pain because sometimes, if my father pays more attention to my stepsisters and my stepbrothers, I feel that he doesn't care about me. Whenever they come down my mother's always buying them whatever food they want. Then, when they drink the stuff that I bought from last week that I've

tried to save, my mother will say that she'll get me more so she can act like a good parent in front of them, so they'll come and live with her. But then she really never buys me anything. She says she will, and she never does.

— *Danielle, 12*

Well, I get jealous of my stepbrother because his father lives down the street, and my father lives in New York. Whenever his father comes around he always takes him out for ice cream or something, and I have to wait for every vacation to see my father, and since we live far apart, we don't really get along. That's hard because I see my brother going around having a good time with his father and I can't.

— *Robin, 12*

The specialist time I've had with my stepsisters is the first day I met them. They started throwing their stuffed animals at me, and I threw them back. It was fun. Just "play fighting."

— *Frankie, 11*

I have one stepbrother, and he goes to visit his real father a lot. My mother divorced his father. They have to work out things like him going away for Christmas and stuff like that. We don't get along very well. I mean, we get along like a brother and sister. We just don't like each other very much, but we get along.

— Erica, 13

No Sibs

"If you break a dish, your parents know it was you."

I like being an only child because I have more space, and I have more privacy. I usually get more privileges because I don't have a brother or sister that would always blame me for things. They'd always say, "Oh, I didn't do it! I didn't do it! Patricia did it! I didn't do it!" And then I'd get blamed, and then I would lose all my privileges. I'm a little more trusted because nobody else is there anyway. I also have more privacy, and that's important to me. I have more space in the bathroom. Sometimes I get lonely because all your friends go on vacation, and you're stuck home, and you don't have anything to do, and you're bored, and you wish somebody was there to talk to or something.

— *Patricia, 12*

I just don't have anybody to stick up for, or anybody to stick up for me. I never had a brother or sister, so I

don't know what it's like. Everybody says that I'm lucky
not to have a brother or sister, though. They say their
brothers and sisters nag them and everything.

— *Robert, 11*

Sometimes, I mean, most of the time, I really wish I
had a younger brother. I don't know why I always wish
for a younger brother. Most people, I think, would ask
for an older sister. But I don't know. I have a half sister
but she didn't spend much time with us. I don't really
remember a lot of it, but I remember I didn't really enjoy
it. I think mainly after that I would prefer a younger
brother, maybe three years younger or something, because I like sports, and so I'd want to help him with that
and stuff. I'd like to teach him what I know and help
him with his homework. Since I'd be the older one, I
could help him get ahead.

— *Kristine, 12*

Whenever I go over my friends' house, all my friends
have brothers or sisters. When I want to invite one of
my friends (who has brothers and sisters) to go to a
movie, her mother usually says to her, "You bring all of
them with you, or none of you goes." That's always a
problem for me. Whenever I go over my friend's house
she has a brother who usually horns in on our playing
time. We don't get enough time in together because he's
always interrupting us. I'm pretty glad I don't have a
brother or sister because I'm afraid that might happen
to me, and none of my friends will like me anymore
because of the problems of having a brother or a sister.

— *Relena, 11*

You might be bored and everything if there's no brothers or sisters around, but a parent sees this and says,
"Well, if he's bored, then why don't we take him out
more often and go to more football games or go to the

fair or get some more stuff for him or something like that?" But they don't spoil me. I just get to go out more often.

— *James, 11*

I think it can be a little bit lonely, but you *do* get out a lot. I suppose I am a bit spoiled, but also your parents treat you like you're really little. You don't get as many privileges. They hold on to you and protect you a lot, they mollycoddle you.

You get a lot of stuff, because if your parents buy something for you they don't have to buy it for your brothers and sisters too, so you get more attention. But I don't like that. I just don't like to get a lot of attention.

— *Patrick, 12*

Brothers and sisters would be a nice thing to have if, like, there's a bully going to pick on you, and your older brother was walking home with you, and he would probably stick up for you. Even an older sister would. And you know you wouldn't be bothered in that particular way.

I know this is sort of mean to say, but when you have this particular chore that you have to do that you don't really like doing, and you have a little brother or sister that really does not mind doing it — in fact he enjoys it because of the extra responsibility that little kids usually want — they will often do it for you, if you ask them nicely, so you can have more time with your friends, instead of them tagging along. Lots of my friends do that with their little brothers and sisters, and their little brothers or sisters are perfectly happy doing it for them.

Having a little brother or sister is not as much of a pain as people say they are. I've often talked to other kids who have brothers and sisters, and they say that when they read books talking about how much of a pain brothers or sisters can be (such as the *Ramona* series by Beverly Cleary) that that is an extremely exaggerated form of what having a little sister is like. They say it isn't at all like that, and you know, they can be fun to have around sometimes.

— *James, 11*

If I had a brother or sister they'd be new in the family, and they'd get all the attention, and I'd be, like, "Huh?!"

— *Stacy, 11*

If you go shopping with your mother you get more clothes because your mother has a lot of money, and she doesn't have to split it up with your sister and yourself, so you get most of it. You get to get more things than your sister does or than your other brothers if you had other brothers.

— *Walter, 12*

It'd be pretty cool not having sisters because you get to do more. You get to do more and ask your mother for money, and she would say, "Sure." She'd not be out of money because your sister just bugged her for ten dollars or something. And I wouldn't have to put up with my sisters' singing or anything.

— Raymond, 12

I think it would be really nice to be an only child because then maybe I could go to camp, because my mother has enough money for maybe two kids or three kids, but four kids want to go. So I would be able to go where I wanted and do more things. I would have my own room instead of sharing one, and I wouldn't always be in fights with my sisters and getting the blame for something I didn't do.

— Colleen, 12

I wouldn't like to be an only child because you get blamed for everything you do. Like, if you broke a dish, your parents are going to know it's you.

— Kiernan, 11

I don't have any sisters or brothers. I don't think it's that good because it means it's only you and your parents, and your parents are really conscious of what you do and how you do in school and how many friends you have. They don't have anyone to compare you to.

— Len, 13

I don't have any brothers or sisters so it gets really lonely sometimes because I have nobody to talk to. Sometimes when I want to talk to somebody my parents either are out or they're off working. But also it's really good I don't have any brothers or sisters because I get to have my parents all to myself, and that's really important to me because my parents are really special. Also, I don't have to share my room with one, and I don't have to share my toys (when I used to have toys) or my books. So it's a lot of fun sometimes. We go on vacation, and sometimes we go out to the music park or something like that.

— Chantrise, 12

Sometime it's kind of boring to have nothing to do. Sometimes I go outside and nobody's outside. I come back in the house and watch TV. Then after TV there is nothing else to do. Then the day is over. I wish I had a brother or sister.

— Leland, 12

I don't have any brothers or sisters. I've heard from friends that they'll hear their brothers snoring, or that their brothers have bad habits and things like that, so I think it's pretty nice to have my own room. Usually you have more space and things like that.

— Jason, 12

If I had a brother or a sister I think they'd be a pain in the neck, especially if they were firstborn because my mother would pay them all the attention, and I want to get a bit of attention. They'd always be telling on me, saying, "Don't touch that because that's mine," or "You're glue and I'm rubber. What you say to me bounces back to you and sticks on you." They would always be telling my mother on me and getting me in trouble, and my mother would be saying, "You know, I told you before not to start any trouble." That's why I don't want any brother. Or a sister.

— Yani, 10

Advice

"Count to ten before you yell."

    If I were to give some advice, I'd tell other kids to expect anything, and deal with problems without blowing your top, and respect other people's ideas, and never have more than two brothers.

— Craig, 14

Count to ten before you yell.

—Amy, 11

    I usually ignore my brother when he does something bad. When I ignore him he's, like, "Oh yeah? You don't want to talk to me?" So if I'm doing a project, like a poster or something, and he comes into the room and goes, "Oops, my hand slipped," and he messes up my poster, and everything falls down, I just keep on ignoring him, and then I just fix up the poster again.

— Kwok Kung, 11

I sometimes bribe my sister. She says, like, "Can I come in your room and watch you do your homework?" I say, "No, I'll give you a present later," so that she doesn't bother me. I never give her anything, though. The best way to get along with your brother and sister is to bribe them.

— *Kenan, 10*

If you're the oldest brother, and you have all little brothers, and if you want to get something out of them, tell them who's the boss, and you know, call them "shorty," or lift them up and stuff like that. If you're the younger brother, just don't go at your bigger brother, because you might get beat up.

— *Miguel, 11*

I don't have a brother or sister, but the advice I'd give to somebody is: Don't have one, and if you do, don't speak to them, because whatever you say gets you in trouble.

— Yani, 10

If you have one, do not *ever* change their diapers, because it's totally disgusting.

— Susan, 10

You tell people to get along with their brothers and sisters just by sharing stuff with them and telling them to share stuff with you. Like, when they want to come in and watch TV, let them come in. Or if they want to listen to your radio, let them listen to it. Then, when they want to wear something of yours, let them wear it. And if they want to go somewhere with you, let them go. Even if they're a pain, even if you're going on a date, let them go.

— Nina, 10

Don't steal things without permission, like clothes or records and stuff like that, because that's a big problem in my house. And if you do borrow them, give them back before your brother or sister gets home. Don't take special things from them and tease them, like take their favorite stuffed animal or something, and throw it up in the air and make it hit the ceiling or something. Just don't take things and don't tease them, I guess.

— Joan, 13

For the middle kids I would usually say you have to think about what the older or younger person feels, because you can't always exclude the younger person just because you think he or she's too young to do everything. You've got to give them credit. Just because the older person is, like, being a little bossy, just think about her because she might be going through some hard times, and you should just, like, ask and see if anything's wrong, but don't ask too much because it will get on their nerves.

— *Robin, 12*

Try to get along with your siblings, older or younger, because if you tattle on them all the time, they can tattle on you, and then you'll never really get to be friends, besides being brother and sister or whatever. If you fight with them all the time, they can blame you for many things, and vice versa, so you'll never really get along. You should try to get along as much as possible, and control yourself on little things. Just don't fight over little itty-bitty things. Just try to control yourself.

— *Eli, 13*

I think that you should always respect them, and even though you might not want to do what they say, like, if it's really stupid, or they ask you to do something for them, then I think you should do it, just to be kind, and I think it would work out better. But if sometimes you don't want to do it, it's okay, and you can get in fights sometimes. Then you work it out and you regret what you did, but you'll still love each other later on.

— *Rebecca, 13*

I would say accept their differences, and as long as they accept yours, don't feel jealous. Don't compare yourself too much to them, because your parents love everybody, and they don't love you any more or any less because you are the youngest. So listen to what they have to say, and don't try to talk too much about their differences or tease them about them.

— *Jennifer, 13*

When you do get into arguments or fights or something, you should try to work them out, not physically, but orally. And you should try to be on their good side

from the start, and not start out with a bad relationship.
Don't start out hating them, but start finding their good
points and go after those instead of being a pessimist
and going, "Oh, my God! Your feet are so *huge!* I hate
big feet!" or something.

— *Jason, 13*

To get along you have to learn each other's problems.
Just learn to live with them, I mean, because that's the
way they are and you have to live with that anyway. So
you just might as well learn to live with it and get along
with each other.

— *Claudia, 13*

Say your brother calls you a name, don't call him one
back. Then he'll go away and you won't get into a fight.
And if you don't want to give something to your sister
because you think she'll break it, don't listen to her if
she calls you a brat, because if you get into a fight you
might get hurt. So don't call them names. Just because
they're calling you names, doesn't mean you have to call
them names.

— *Nancy, 12*

I used to always get in fights with my older brother.
After a while I learned that if I cooperated with him he'd
say, "All right, no problem." It's really helpful to just
cooperate, and every once in a while you can ask him
to do a favor. Sometimes they oblige, sometimes they
don't . . . you just gotta go with the flow.

— *Mark, 12*

If you have a younger brother, one thing to do is to
teach him things. I was sharpening one of my knives
once, and then my brother came in, and he looked interested. He started asking me questions about why I
put oil on it, and then I showed him why you do that,

and I told him what happens if you don't and everything. Then, we got along better . . . for about an hour.

— *Joel, 11*

If your sister is starting to get on your case, and she keeps bothering you about the same thing, just don't let her finish the sentence. Just say, "Yeah, you're right" or something. Then she'll get all mad, and she'll feel like you're not listening to her. So then you really get the best of her instead of her getting the best of you. She'll say something like, "I have better things to do than argue with you" or something.

— *Michael, 11*

If you're having trouble with your sisters or something, you could try to talk to them about it or try to be a little nicer to them, and maybe they'll be nicer to you. I try that, but they don't usually give me a chance 'cause they make faces at me when I'm trying to do it.

— *John, 11*

This might not be the case for everyone, but my sister usually gets mad at me because I've done something to her in the past. So, sometimes you can just start being nice and maybe she'll stop. I tried that once and it worked. I just stopped hitting her and telling her to be quiet and stuff like that. So she stopped singing and bossing me around . . . for about two or three hours.

— *Ben, 11*

If your brother or sister comes in the house mad and everything, calling you names, just ignore them and finish what you're doing, like watching TV or something. If they keep doing it, just kick 'em. That'll get them out of the house.

— *Kristine, 11*

If my sister looks really glum or sad, I always try and make her laugh . . . like, I go "Ahhh Ha Ha Ha Ha" . . . I like to make people laugh.

— *David, 11*

Don't bug your sisters or brothers about things that they don't want to tell you, 'cause then you'll just end up getting in lots of fights. If they tell you something they don't want you to tell, don't tell other people.

— *Liz, 11*

My advice to kids that have younger brothers or older brothers or sisters is to try to get along with them, you know, try to understand their part of being, like, try to understand why they do things, not just go along and hit them or get in a fight with them or something. And if they did something real wrong, just try to help 'em out. That's my advice to all of you.

— *Rudi, 12*

My advice to kids is try and understand when your brothers and sisters tell you what to do that all they want to do is help you. Try and understand that when they pick on you, they want to teach you how to fight. But,

you should never fight with your older brother or little brothers or sisters because that's not right, because you might need them.

— Dora, 12

I just say that you should *try* to ignore them, try as hard as you can. Maybe you *should* hit your brother or sister just for good measure. I don't know. I just *can't* ignore them sometimes.

— Danielle, 12

Try to understand your older sisters because they're older. I know they're supposed to boss you around and everything, but just try to cooperate with them, and just try not to annoy them, and try not to get them mad or anything. Act as a family, as you're supposed to.

A family is supposed to stick together, help one another. And if one is sick, try to help them, try to cure them. And, you know, when you need help on homework and certain stuff like that, just try to act as a real family, not argue all the time.

— Marisol, 13